Wilderness like Eden

Richard Fellows

WordWyze Publishing

Copyright © 2019 by Richard Fellows

WILDERNESS LIKE EDEN

All rights reserved.

First Published 2019

Richard Fellows reserves the moral right to be identified
as the author of this work.

Short extracts and brief quotations,
may be copied for non-profit personal use only, without prior permission.

Otherwise, no part of this publication may be reproduced,
stored in a retrieval system, or transmitted in any form or by any means,
electronic, mechanical, photocopying, scanning or otherwise,
without the prior written consent of the author.

Cover Photos: Dreamstime.com, ©Miguel Nicolaevsky; pixabay,
CoolCatGameStudio

Cover Design: Bettina Kradolfer

Co-Published by: WordWyze Publishing

Most Scripture references are from the New King James Version. Copyright ©
1982 by Thomas Nelson, Inc. Used by permission. All rights reserved.

Printed Soft-cover edition: ISBN 978-0-648-58830-6

Epub Edition: ISBN 978-0-648-58831-3

DEDICATION

To Joanna Taylor,

A lady whom I honour and respect greatly. You were prayer-covering me, long before I ever met you or knew you existed, and for that, I am truly thankful. Since crossing paths, you have greatly strengthened me and helped me through many seasons.

You are a forerunner who has shown me the closeness and realness of the Kingdom. But above all, I thank you with all my heart for being a faithful prayer warrior – Your prayers move mountains. You are one of a few that fulfil James 5:16, "The effective, fervent prayer of a righteous [daughter] of the Most High avails much." Such power and closeness to the Lord!

I honour you, Joanna…

To Bettina Kradolfer, you are an amazing and true friend for life. Thank you so much for the fantastic Cover and Artwork for this Book.

Dedicated to Jesus, my Lord – Without you, I am nothing! Your love is uncontainable, so powerful, and too beautiful to put in words. This book is for You and Your glory.

My heart and soul are Yours, and all glory goes to Your Name.

FOREWORD

It is a joy to write this Foreword for my friend, Richard Fellows.

I have known Richard for nearly twenty-five years, and we have shared many Kingdom conversations and experiences together. Richard is a unique person with an inquisitive mind that seeks to understand truth through the revelation of God's Word. Richard is also carrying an inner freedom that allows him to go beyond the familiar and seek out hidden Kingdom treasures.

Over the past decade, there has been an increasing global focus towards the Kingdom of Heaven. The phrase "On earth as it is in Heaven" spoken by Jesus himself, as part of the Lord's Prayer, has become a commonly used phrase in prayers, declarations, sermons and worship songs around the earth. As the Holy Spirit is drawing the body of Christ towards a renewed focus on Heaven, the effects are beginning to be seen on a whole new level.

> *"Faith is the substance of things hoped for and the evidence of things unseen." (Hebrews 11:1)*

One of the effects of this increasing union of the two realms, is the physical manifestation of Heavenly things on earth. We are in a day in which spiritual essence is becoming "substance" and "evidence". Stones out of Heaven are at the front of this manifestation.

I personally have seen many hundreds of stones of different colours, shapes and compositions appear supernaturally during a revival amongst children in a remote part of India. Children testified to holding stones in their hands in a spiritual form while in Heaven, only to have them manifest in a physical form when they return to earth. It was when Richard experienced these miraculous events that his inquisitive mind began a six-year research journey that is now captured in this book.

Wilderness like Eden is a combination of sound Biblical scholarship and historical research combined with current revelation, supportive testimony and revelatory insight. I believe this work is very timely and stands as a forerunning theology regarding the manifestation of Heavenly elements on the earth.

What you will glean from this book is that the manifestation of gemstones out of Heaven is not a new phenomenon but is very much woven throughout Biblical history and the Kingdom journey. We can expect that as Heaven and earth continue to join together at an increasing rate, that the manifestation of Heaven's stones will become even more common throughout the earth, as communities of people come into Heavenly freedom.

Wilderness like Eden will also help to settle the sceptics who hold to the foundation of Biblical truth but have not found clear reference to this kind of manifestation in Scripture and question the power by which these manifestations are occurring.

For the Lord says in Isaiah 45:3,

> *"I will give you hidden treasure, riches from secret places, so that you may know that I Am the Lord, the God of Israel, who summons you by name."*

We believe that the Lord wants to restore the earth to its former glory. Through the sacrifice of Christ upon the cross, all grace is available to the body and bride of Christ to progressively journey towards the reconciliation of Heaven and earth, through love and intimacy. We believe that stones manifesting out of Heaven are a visible witness of this growing intimacy, union and love.

"For the Lord will comfort Zion, He will comfort all her waste places, He will make her wilderness like Eden, And her desert like the garden of the Lord. Joy and gladness will be found in it, Thanksgiving and the voice of melody." (Isaiah 51:3)

Let Eden be re-established on earth and let Heaven's stones stand as a forerunning witness of our growing union with the Kingdom of Heaven and our Heavenly Bridegroom.

Jason Cobb   - *The Life Foundation, New Zealand, 2019*

Contents

DEDICATION iii
FOREWORD v
PREFACE xi
CHAPTER ONE 13
   Manifesting Gemstones 13
      So, what is this phenomenon? 14
      How does it happen? 15
      What is the Veil? 16
      Why is it important? 16
      My Story 17
CHAPTER TWO 25
   Are You Out of Your Mind? Biblical Scholarship 25
CHAPTER THREE 37
   They came down from Heaven! Jewish Rabbis 37
CHAPTER FOUR 45
   Controversy, Glassy, Plastic, Fake – Not so Fast! 45
CHAPTER FIVE 53
   The Creation Covenant 53
CHAPTER SIX 59
   The Priest Adorned with Jewels 59
CHAPTER SEVEN 69
   The Bride Adorned with Her Jewels 69
CHAPTER EIGHT 77
   Not just a Priest, a Bride, but also a King! 77

CHAPTER NINE	85
Kings, Lions, Dragons, and Stones	85
CHAPTER TEN	91
Symbolic Memorial Stones!	91
CHAPTER ELEVEN	95
Stones of Function: Lion, Man, Ox, Eagle	95
CHAPTER TWELVE	103
The Full Face of God in Stone	103
CHAPTER THIRTEEN	107
The Eternal Breastplate - The City on the Heart of God	107
CHAPTER FOURTEEN	115
Stones of Fire: Hidden in the Heartbeat of God	115
CHAPTER FIFTEEN	131
Store Up Your Treasures in Your Heavenly Account	131
CHAPTER SIXTEEN	139
Teardrop Gemstones	139
CHAPTER SEVENTEEN	145
Multi-dimensional Revelation Stones of Glory!	145
CHAPTER EIGHTEEN	151
Eden, Garden, Tabernacle in the Wilderness, and the Church	151
CHAPTER NINETEEN	159
The Full Council of Scripture	159
CHAPTER TWENTY	175
Concluding Appeal & Whereto from Here?	175
BIBLIOGRAPHY	181

PREFACE

This book is birthed out of experiencing an incredible season of the Kingdom of Heaven manifesting on earth (2014). I'm talking about realms of the Kingdom materializing before my eyes from another world to touch and hold, in the form of gemstones, as if out of thin air.

These manifestations were a tangible representation of God's revelatory glory. To behold God's glory and revelation in precious stones. These experiences deeply smashed my box of reality, the total fabric of what I thought was possible, and also showed me how close God's love can interact with us. As I tried to process what I had seen (many times over), and been told by some people, that the Bible says nothing about gemstones manifesting, I decided to search the internet for answers. Back then (six years ago), all I could find was a website that gave two passages on stones that I really didn't think held much water in making a justification for them appearing.

I knew what I had seen, received and held in my hands, in the midst of great Kingdom presence. I was not going to give up, so this book is my journey of six years' researching the Bible, Jewish authorities, Rabbi's writings and Biblical Scholars on the knowledge of manifesting gemstones from Heaven. I have also spent time dialoguing with people around the world who have had similar experiences.

The Bible, in fact, has a lot to say about gemstones. Many say, "Where does the Bible talk about gemstones"? And my short reply is, "In Heaven, God's Throne, the Stones of Fire, Lucifer's covering, the Crystal Sea flowing down into the river of Pishon in the Garden, to Adam's covering, to Moses' Stones from the Throne, to the Priest's Urim & Thummim Stones, to the Priest's breastplate, to the adorning of Function Stones for the Priests, Brides, Lords and Kings, to the Reward Stones in the walls of salvation, to the Memorial Stones, to Teardrop Stone, to the Overcomers' Stones."

The Jews have a saying, "It rained down manna and precious stones in the wilderness". There is a deep tapestry and belief in this claim, and once you perceive the tapestry it is like a key in the kingdom that unlocks the universe.

When God divided the firmament of the waters and created the universe, He entered a covenant with creation, a marriage covenant. Creation was cut out of Heaven to be and become His bride. The Tabernacle was also called the bride, and also the twelve tribes of Israel were called the bride. And Believers today are also called the bride of Christ.

If God adorns His bride with precious stones, then the adorning will manifest in Creation, in Eden, the Wilderness, the Tabernacle, the Temple, the Church, and on the people of God. Creation will be filled with the glory of the manifold wisdom of God. If we are priests, lords, and kings functioning in God's kingdom, then we should expect to be adorned with the Kingdom being manifested in the earth.

This book is written for those who have stood in the trenches of God's unfolding Kingdom and been heavily criticized by these manifestations. For it has come from a lack of knowledge and Biblical research.

This book is also written for those who are hungry to understand the revelation of the stones. For the stones speak of us and our representation as the image of God. I pray that this book brings understanding and revelation and wonder. I believe there is more to learn, and more will be revealed in years to come.

Richard Fellows (2019)

CHAPTER ONE

Manifesting Gemstones

In this book, my aim is to lay a systematic, theological foundation to the significance of the "Gemstone Phenomenon" that is happening around the world. It is Scripture-based and written with research, testimonies and bullet points to capture all angles of understanding. In this Chapter, I wish to lay a foundation of the "True" reality of this phenomenon, grounding it with eye-witness accounts and testimonies.

SO, WHAT IS THIS PHENOMENON?

This phenomenon is that gemstones are appearing/ manifesting (You could say out of thin air) in meetings/Churches where intense worship and the Lord's presence is abiding. They are also appearing in people's homes where the atmosphere of Heaven is being cultivated.

Reports of Gemstones suddenly appearing at random locations while faithful worshipers soak in the presence of God, have brought many questions to the minds of sceptics and Believers alike. Why are these supernatural gemstones manifesting, and what is their significance? Many are asking why would God manifest gemstones; what has this got to do with Christianity or the Gospel? These are the questions I intend to answer in this book. Before I had my own experience that shattered my "box" of reality, seeing this manifestation happen many times over a period of seven weeks, I had little knowledge that the Bible even spoke about gemstones. But since my experiences, I have set out over the last six years to study everything the Bible says about them, and I have been blown away on how much the Bible speaks on gemstones and their significance. I have read a couple of books from others who have set out to write on this manifestation, but I have found they have been very faint on explaining a "theology" and context for them. I do believe the Lord has given me insights and revelations that I have not seen or read elsewhere. So, I set out to detail and explain the gemstone manifestation, their revelation, and why it is happening in our timeline in God.

For many, they just see gemstones and nothing else (no context or significance), but with God and His ways, everything has layers and layers of revelation. The stones have a complete Theology and speak forth a revelation. It is not about their value, that's not the focus (some are very valuable in earthly terms, and some are not). Earthly value is not their ultimate purpose: the stones are a carrier of revelation before they are anything else. They reflect layers and dimensions of revelation about us and our place in God's Kingdom. As the Chapters unfold, we will see that our lives carry significance, and the greater significance and victories we have, greater glory is cut into the stones to behold.

> *Coming to Him, as to a living stone, rejected indeed by men, but chosen by God and precious, you also, as living stones, are being built up a spiritual house, a holy priesthood, to offer up spiritual sacrifices acceptable to God through Jesus Christ. (1 Peter 2:4-5)*

HOW DOES IT HAPPEN?

There are two ways the gemstones appear/manifest. I will explain one way here and the other a little later in this Chapter. The first way they appear, is that Angels bring them and push them through the spiritual veil to manifest. Angels are ministering spirits that bring things to us to equip us.

> *Are they not all ministering spirits sent forth to minister for those who will inherit salvation. (Hebrews 1:14)*

Angels activate healings, bring food, open prison doors, protect us, and bring us revelation.

WHAT IS THE VEIL?

The Veil is the boundary of separation, between the spiritual realm and the earthly world of physical matter. The world we see with our human eyes is the physical world, and on the other side is the spiritual world.

> *This Hope we have as an anchor of the soul, both sure and steadfast, and which enters the Presence behind the Veil. (Hebrews 6:19)*

> *Therefore, brethren having boldness to enter the holiest by the blood of Jesus, by a new and living way, through the veil, He consecrated for us with His flesh." (Hebrews 10:19) Behind the Veil is the spiritual world, and we have access to the Kingdom and Heaven through the door, which is Jesus. (John 10:9)*

WHY IS IT IMPORTANT?

The Bible is full of a "Gemstone Theology". We cannot be ignorant, for they speak layers of revelation to us.

The manifesting stones can bring controversy; a number of people have seen them and criticized them. To the sceptic, who is always questioning their value, Scripture is clear that not all the stones were of great value, many different stones were used in God's House.

> *Now for the house of my God I have prepared with all my might: gold for things to be made from gold, silver for things to be made from silver, bronze for things of bronze, iron for things of iron, wood for things of wood, onyx stones, stones to be set, glistening stones of various colours, all kinds of precious stones and marble slabs in abundance. (1 Chronicles 29:2)*

MY STORY

My first exposure to the Gemstone manifesting reality, started when I went to visit a friend who ran an Orphanage in the jungles of India. They had just been through great persecution, and the Lord had started to visit them in a very powerful way. The Holy Spirit came in incredible power and presence, and the children in worship would be taken over by the Holy Spirit and caught up into trances (Acts 10:10) and visions of Heaven (Acts 7:55). When the Holy Spirit came upon them, they would go into visions and fall on the floor as if they were asleep. When they woke up, they would get up and retell the wonders they had seen in Heaven with Jesus. Now, one may say: "STOP RIGHT THERE, this is just hallucinations, this proves nothing!"

BUT, what does one say, when a child is on the floor in a vision, (I'm sitting next to them, and their hand is open and empty), and as they awaken, you see their hand close tightly shut; then as they stand to their feet and declare that "Jesus gave them a gemstone in Heaven", and on opening their hand, the stone is sparkling on their palm? It is a little harder to deny. This I saw many times... I saw it in India and in New Zealand. I've even seen children come out of visions, open their mouths and gemstones fall out. I've also been in houses and seen them appear before my eyes all through the house.

Psalms 81:10 says,

> *I am the Lord your God, who brought you out of the land of Egypt: open your mouth wide, and I will fill it.*

In his book, *The Treasury of David*, Charles Spurgeon indicates that "an ancient custom of Persian Kings was to invite honoured guests to open wide their mouths, so the King could cram them with sweetmeats. If he was particularly pleased with an individual, jewels would sometimes be included in the mouthful."[1]

I have seen it so many times now, that I know there is no magic, deceit or falseness about this phenomenon.

I was once in New Zealand, standing in a park, and I felt the Holy Spirit come upon me. As I turned around, I saw a man sitting on a bench. I felt led to go over to him and share some of my experiences. Just as I was about to leave, I looked down on the ground and by his foot was a gemstone, which had manifested. I picked it up and gave it to him as confirmation of what I had just been sharing.

Linda Cruz in her book, *All His Jewels: From Glory to Glory*, writes,

> "Labor Day weekend of 2006, I attended a conference in Nashville, Tennessee, where I interviewed several attendees about this new phenomenon. At least two people related personal stories to me of jewels manifesting. The leader of the conference, Jeff Jansen, showed me a ruby that supernaturally appeared in one of his meetings. As he held it in the palm of his hand, I observed its dark red colour and faceted face."[2]

This stone appeared/manifested in his hand in one of his meetings.

Mary Trask in her book, *The 12 Gemstones of Revelation: Unlocking The Significance of the Gemstone Phenomenon*, writes,

> "Glenn, a middle-aged businessman, sat before his home computer taking care of some necessary work

---

[1] Mary Trask, *The 12 Gemstones of Revelation: Unlocking The Significance of the Gemstones Phenomenon*, Destiny Image, 2009, p.18
[2] Linda Cruz, *All His Jewels*, Xulon Press, 2007, p.4

related to his accounting business in the Seattle, Washington, area. Suddenly, he sensed the presence of the Lord in his office. He stopped what he was working on and began freely worshipping the Lord with childlike abandon. In the midst of his worship, Glenn heard something drop to the floor, so he stopped to investigate. Directly outside of his office door, he peered down to discover three walnut-sized, precision cut gemstones sitting on the floor. One of the gemstones appeared to be a purple amethyst…meanwhile in Redding, California, young David and his wife Taylor had just returned from a prayer meeting where small, perfectly cut diamonds had been found in the carpet of the home where they and others had gathered to pray. Later that same night, as they prepared for bed, they pulled back the bed covers to find a large, heart-shaped diamond resting atop the middle of their mattress. Curious, they brought the large diamonds to a gemmologist for examination. After studying the flawless stone, he promptly offered them $10,000 for the diamond."[3]

Mary Trask goes on to write,

"In the Puget Sound region of Washington, Leola reported that the small collection of gemstones she had found in her home, and at several different services throughout 2008, appeared to be increasing in size." And also, "At a small church in Colville, Washington, it was reported that, even as the preacher stood in the front of the sanctuary, several eyewitnesses saw gemstones appearing mid-air before dropping to the floor. An estimated 200 gemstones, some of which were amethysts, were collected in a single morning service."[4]

---

[3] Trask, p.15.
[4] Trask, p.150.

John Crowder in his book, *The Ecstasy of Loving God,* writes,

> "We have watched diamonds grow, even doubling in size on rings (sometimes when this happens, it breaks the metal prongs). We have seen gemstones turn colours, as the Lord changes the substance and adds value to the stones. But it seems the Lord is pulling out all stops in this hour. He will not be satisfied with just a few gemstones falling. When God shows up, He shows out. At the time of this writing, more than 40 perfectly cut 50-carat gemstones have recently fallen at a church in Coeur D' Alene, Idaho. These have been dropped by angels, and the estimated value on some of these has ranged up to $20 million individually. In addition, there are resident glory portals opening in some locations today, where there have been hundreds of large and small gemstones, sequins and flecks of onyx supernaturally appearing."[5]

I have heard over the years that Charlie Shamp, from Destiny Encounters, has received gemstones in his meetings; Rob Deluca has received gemstones manifesting in his Church; Ian Clayton of Sons of Thunder Ministries has had a gemstone manifest/come out of his hand (will explain this more, later in the book, hint for now - "The Kingdom of God is within You"); Justin Paul Abrahams from Company of Burning Hearts Ministries, has had them manifest and appear in his house. Now, this occurrence is not just happening around the lives of top Christian Leaders, it's also happening to simple, genuine, unknown Believers all around the world. I've even heard of a guy who received some gemstones and sold them for $6000 to buy a van to go around and preach the Gospel.

I have seen documentation from a guy called Jason Cuellar, who wanted to silence sceptics about his gemstones, showing a report

---

5   John Crowder, *The Ecstasy of Loving God*, Destiny Image, 2009, P.231.

from a Gemmologist, who confirmed all were real stones and had a price value of $3500.

Many of the stones that appear are not of great earthly value. Many just look like glassy stones. Scripture calls these "glistening stones" (1 Chronicles 29:2). And no, they weren't bought from China or some online-shop. These small glass stones I have seen change colour and grow in size and pulsate with presence. Isaiah 54:11-12 describes our foundations and walls as being adorned with "colourful gems" and precious stones. So, we have different grades (glories) of stones in Scripture, colourful gems, glistening stones, and precious stones. Also, the Lord is very careful about people's hearts and knows that people can idolize the stones and not open their heart fully to the Giver of the stone (Himself) who gives perfect gifts from above (James 1:17). The Lord's purpose of the stones is the revelation they carry, not ultimately their value. As I have said already, there are many stones manifesting today that are valuable, but the Lord tests people's hearts.

> *"For where your treasure is, there your heart will be also."*
> *(Matthew 6:21)*

It is their revelation that is mind-blowing! (Theology)

This manifestation cannot be labelled "Fake", or "People are just dropping stones on the ground". No, No, No, this is not what is happening: too many people have seen them appear before their eyes.

Here are some more testimonies from simple, genuine Believers that I know personally,

Ben Lewis:

> "After Richy came back from India and told me about gemstones, I was fascinated, so I started to declare and pray for them to manifest in my house. About a year

later, I found my first one and was blown away. The second one I found, appeared in our prayer room. It literally was not there one minute and then the next, I saw it shining and picked it up. I have found three so far. For me, it's a sign from God saying, 'I can do anything, do you believe?'"

Judy Abrahams:

"A couple of years ago when Jason and Jo visited my house, some of the grandkids came, and gems started showing up on the stairs and in the kid's room upstairs; small clear ones and coloured ones. We called friends with kids and gave each one a small plastic bag, and they all found about ten each. We called more friends and more got found. One granddaughter said, 'Nanny I want a purple one.' I said, 'Ask Jesus.' She did, and a few minutes later, she came to me saying she had found two purple ones. One of my friends had been earlier in the day saying she wanted a purple one. So, I told my Danika, 'You need to give one of your purple ones to Penny,' who was her neighbour. So, she did. Jo said that altogether that day, 280 gems came through into my house. God is so cool."

Sjaan Rounds:

"Ruby just found another gem at school the other day in the toilets. This is her third, I think, that she has found at school. But when we were putting it away with the others, we noticed our little blue one, that Pat found by my feet had changed to a light green colour! So amazing! It wasn't long after, I read about yours changing colour."

Fiona Dieleman:

"It had been a rather challenging morning at church, and I had been doubting my own discernment and feeling a little bit discouraged. That evening, I was the first person into the prayer room for the prayer meeting and was arranging some chairs, when a small sparkle against the wall caught my eye. It was a reasonably big purple/pink gemstone, not the full-on sparkly kind, but I knew it was from the Lord, nonetheless, letting me know that He was in the midst of my day and my discouragement."

Jason Cobb:

"On the 21st of October, 2009, following persecution, focused prayer and heightened praise, the Holy Spirit visited our community in an extraordinary way. The spiritual eyes of the believing children in our Children's Home were miraculously opened, and they were caught up into Heaven, an experience that has continued on a near-daily basis, since then. From the early days, the children tried to bring back from their visits to Heaven, many kinds of Heavenly treasures, including Heavenly stones. We saw many looks of bewilderment on the faces of returning children, as the stones that were so real in the spiritual Kingdom were now not present in this natural world. We prompted them to ask Jesus about this. In Heaven, Jesus told a group of visiting children, 'Keep praying, one day they will come through.' It took two years of focused prayer before the breakthrough came.

"One night, when we were having our regular Heaven prayer, our daughter walked up to my wife and I with her eyes closed, while in a Heavenly trance. She said, 'Mum, this is from Jesus.' She then opened her hand and in it was a beautifully faceted stone, resembling a diamond. She then closed her hand and came over to me and said, 'Dad, this is from Jesus.' She then opened her hand again, and there was a second stone of the same shape and size. When she returned from her Heavenly experience, she confirmed that Jesus had personally given her two stones to deliver to my wife and I. She was overwhelmed with joy to learn that the stones had actually come through after many months of trying. Before our very eyes, we witnessed an amazing miracle, the spiritual substance had become a physical substance. Following this initial manifestation, our community has had the joy of seeing many hundreds of stones transition from Heaven to earth."

> *"O, you afflicted one, tossed with tempest, and not comforted. Behold, I will lay your stones with colourful gems, and lay your foundations with sapphires. I will make your pinnacles of rubies, Your gates of crystal, and all your walls of precious stones. All your children shall be taught by the Lord, and great shall be the peace of your children." (Isaiah 54:11-13)*

CHAPTER TWO

Are You Out of Your Mind? Biblical Scholarship

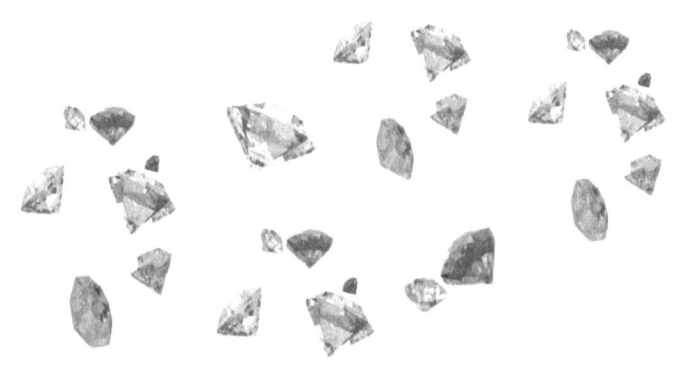

Many will say, "Are you out of your mind?"; "What has this got to do with the Bible?"; "Nowhere in the Bible does it talk about gemstones manifesting." People may be surprised to learn that the Bible actually says a lot about gemstones, from Genesis to Revelation. Before we look at the Biblical evidence in the Bible, I would like to quote Jewish Rabbis and Biblical Scholars on the subject of manifesting gemstones. You may be not so sceptical, when you read that those closest to the texts, and those with the sharpest minds, are not "out of their minds" when they conclude gemstones manifested from Heaven.

Rabbi Ari Enkin, Rabbinic Director of the *United with Israel*, says,

> "For those unfamiliar, there were very few grocery stores, restaurants and bakeries in the Sinai desert back then (and today too!). But the more than one million Jewish people had to eat during the 40 years of wandering in the desert. So, God sent manna down from Heaven each day (except on Shabbat), which was a bread-like food that sustained them.
>
> "Not many people know this, but the *Midrash* (rabbinic literature) teaches that along with the daily allotted loaf of manna, came…jewellery! That's right. The manna was accompanied by diamonds and other precious stones. Now get this: The Midrash continues by saying "the greatest" people (referring to the leaders) went right for the jewels, while "the simple folk" cared about the manna.
>
> "Rabbi Michel Twerski of Milwaukee notes that the financial and economic situation of the Jewish people in the desert was very unique: they had no needs. Everything was taken care off. Their food fell from Heaven. They were accompanied by 'Miriam's well', which provided fresh water at all times. Their clothing never wore out. There was no disease or illness. God

ensured that the weather was always comfortable. If one has no needs or expenses, then what was the use of the precious stones? Who would trade them? Where were they to be deposited? What would they be used to buy? Indeed, it may very well be that ultimately, the precious stones were completely useless! Precious stones in the deserts would have about as much value as sand in a desert or snow in the Arctic.

"The answer, it is explained, is that 'great people' see far beyond the here and now. The 'great people' knew, or were at least anticipating, that one day there would be a *Mishkan* (Tabernacle) and a *Beit Hamilkdash* (Holy Temple), where a High Priest would need precious stones as part of his breastplate. These leaders were not collecting the precious stones due to some kind of materialistic obsession. Rather, they were collecting due to their sensitivity to the spiritual needs of a nation."[1]

"This account also appears in the *Midrash* (Shemot Rabba 33:8), which adds that "the leaders among them would come and collect them and hid them." The *gedolim*, the prominent members of the nation, collected these precious jewels and hide them until they were needed for the priestly garments. The Yefei Toar commentary to the *Midrash* explains this to mean that the precious stones fell only with the portions of manna intended for these prominent individuals, and this is why only they collected the jewels. Alternatively, the Yefei Toar suggests, Moshe (Moses) perhaps issued a specific directive authorizing only these leaders to collect the precious stones."[2]

---

1 Rabbi Ari Enkin, (2015 January), *Living Torah: Leaving Egypt and Looking to the Future,* http://Unitedwithisrael.org/living-torah-leaving-egypt-and-looking-to-the-future/
2 Enklin

The Scholar G.K. Beale says,

> "According to Jewish tradition, precious stones fell along with the manna" (cf. Midr. Psalms 78:4).[3]

This phenomenon is not new or made up, but genuinely Biblical.

Yoma 75a:19, a treatise in the *Mishnah* and *Talmud*, says,

"With regard to donations for the Tabernacle, the verse states: 'And they brought yet to him freewill offerings every morning' (Exodus 36:3). The *Gemara* asks: 'what is the meaning of 'every morning'? Rabbi Shmuel Bar Nahmani said that Rabbi Yonatan said: 'They brought donations from that which fell every morning with the manna.' This teaches that pearls and precious stones fell for the Israelites with the manna. It states: 'And the rulers (nesi'im) brought the onyx stones' (Exodus 35:27). A *Tanna* taught that the word *nesi'im* means actual clouds brought them. As it states: 'As clouds (nesi'im) and winds without rain, so is he that boasts himself of a false gift" (Proverbs 25:14). We learn from this that the precious stones fell from the clouds with the manna."[4]

The Biblical Scholar Sam Storms says,

> "John's thought is no doubt drawn to the manna (speaking of Revelation 2:17), because of the allusion to Balaam, in whose time Israel was being fed with manna from Heaven, and according to Jewish tradition, precious stones fell along with the manna."[5]

---

[3] G.K.Beale, *The Book of Revelation: A Commentary on the Greek Text*. Grand Rapids: Paternoster Press, 1999, p.252-253.
[4] http://sefaria.org/Yoma.75a.19
[5] Sam Storms, n.d. *The Letter to The Church at Pergamum (2:12-17)*.

The Catholic Scholar Stephen Beale (this is not G.K. Beale noted above) – says,

> "Moreover, according to ancient Jewish tradition, precious stones and pearls rained down from Heaven along with the manna. Precious stones also adorned the vestments for priests in ancient Israel. The connection the precious stones suggest, between manna and priestly vestments, makes sense if we remember that the manna is a type of Eucharist, the Body of Christ, the perfect priest who has sacrificed Himself for us."[6]

Dr. Michael Heiser, in his book, *The Unseen Realm*, says:

> "Based on parallels found in Second Temple Jewish literature, the white stone was a symbol of legal acquittal or a token of membership among the righteous. Second Baruch 29:8 says, 'And it will happen again at that time that the treasury of manna will come down again from on high, and they will eat of it in those years because these are they who have arrived at the consummation.' Accordingly, the white stone becomes the invitation to take part in Jesus' Supper. The notion of that being a banquet meal is supported by the reference to "manna". According to Jewish tradition, precious stones fell along with the manna (cf. Midr Ps 78.4). According to another Jewish tradition, these priestly stones were stored in a hidden ark, to be revealed in messianic times." (cf 2 Bar 6:7-8).[7]

---

6   Stephen Beale, (Nov 2017) *Why do Christians Get White Stones in Heaven?*
7   Michael S. Heiser, The Unseen Realm: Recovering the supernatural worldview of the Bible, Lexham Press, 2015, p.381.

The above shows us that Jewish Rabbis and Jewish Writings and Biblical Scholars believe "Precious Stones" fell from Heaven, with the manna in the wilderness.

But there is more: Jewish tradition and Scripture hint that Moses also received stones from Heaven. When Moses received the Law of God on Mount Sinai, God Himself wrote upon the tablets of stone with His finger. These stones were not clay stones, (at least not the first ones), but Sapphire stones, cut out of the throne of glory. According to the Jewish Midrash, the tablets of stone were made from blue Sapphire as a symbol of the Heavens and God's throne.

> "Moses departed from the Heavens with two tablets on which the Ten Commandments were engraved and they were made of Sapphire like stone." (L.Ginzberg: Legends of the Jews Vol 3:118)[8]

> "The Sapphire, used for the tablets, was taken from the throne of Glory." (Vol 6:49)[9]

Rabbinical Judaism, as found in the Talmud and Mishnah, teaches that the tablets of the Law were made of Sapphire. In the Law, Jewish men were required to place tassels on the four corners of their garments and insert a permanent blue thread in all four corners of the prayer shawl (Numbers 15:38). The tassels and the blue thread (techelet) were a reminder to remember God's Commandments that he gave to Israel (Numbers 15:39).

> "Why does the Torah enjoin us regarding techelet? Because techelet resembles sapphire, and the tablets were made of sapphire, to tell you that as long as Bnei Yisrael gaze upon this techelet, they are reminded of what is

---

8 Dinah Dye, The Temple Revealed In Creation, A Portrait Of The Family, Foundation in Torah Publishing, 2016, p.57

9 Dye, p.57.

inscribed on the tablets and observe the commandments. Therefore, it is written, 'And you shall see (the techelet string) and remember all of the commandments of God, and you shall do them.'" (Mishnat Rabbi Eliezer)

God gave Moses Stones from Heaven!

One Jewish Commentary says, speaking about the Urim and Thummim stones (which hid inside the breastplate of the High Priest), and communicated the Lord's Will and lit up the other stones with a message of letters that,

> "The Urim & Thummim did not belong in the physical world, they were not from this world. Nachmanides, likewise, describes the (stones in) parchment as "the handiwork of Heaven", and "a secret handed to Moses from the mouth of the Almighty."[10]

These stones were clearly Supernatural Stones!

In the Apocryphal book of Enoch, it tells us that Heaven has plenty of precious stones. The book of Enoch was considered by many early Church Fathers to be inspired by God and in the Canon of Scripture:

> *8. I perceived at the extremity of the earth the firmament of heaven above it. Then I passed on towards the south;*
>
> *9. Where burnt, both by day and night, six mountains formed of glorious stones; three towards the east, and three towards the south.*
>
> *10. Those which were towards the east were of a variegated stone; one of which was of margarite, and another of antimony. Those*

---

10 Rabbi Dovid Rosenfeld, (n.d.) Urim and Thummim. http://www.aish.com/atr/Urim-and-Thummim.html.

towards the south were of a red stone. The middle one reached to heaven like the throne of God; a throne composed of alabaster, the top of which was of sapphire." (Enoch 18:8-10)[11]

In the Testament of Solomon, a Pseudepigraphal work (1st – 2nd century), it describes the angel Michael giving Solomon a powerful ring from Heaven, with an engraved precious stone on it. Now, whether this story is true or false (most likely a legend) is not my point. My point of including it is to show "that at least the idea, the concept" of an angel bringing precious stones down, was in the minds of Jewish thinkers. The concept was not non-existent but existed whether true or false. Now some may say "this is magical rings" kind of stuff. But before we judge too fast, didn't a "Snake-shaped hunk of metal" which Moses made and held up, heal people in the wilderness? There was an anointing on it.

Biblical Scholar Darrel L. Bock says "In 1 Enoch, he is named (Michael) as one of the angels who watch, along with Gabriel and others. His function here is said to extend over people and nations. In the slightly later Testament of Solomon 1:6, Michael, an archangel, gives Solomon a ring with a seal engraved on a precious stone that allows him to face the demonic forces. The gift is said to come from the Lord in Heaven."

Chapter 8 of the book of Enoch assigns certain teaching to specific angels, "Moreover Azazyel taught men to make swords, knives, shields, breastplates, the fabrication of mirrors, and the workmanship of bracelets and ornaments, the use of paint, the beautifying of the eyebrows, the use of stones of every valuable and select kind, and of all sorts of dyes, so that the world became altered.

It would appear that individual angels had expertise in particular areas. Enoch, in this chapter and context, is referring to the actions

---

[11] https://book-ofenoch.com/chapter-18/

of fallen angels, but this does not discredit what angels can do. Men learned how to make weapons, thus introducing war. The women learned how to beautify themselves, which immediately leads to fornication. It was not the bringing down of the stones or having knowledge of making bracelets and ornaments with precious stones, that was the sin; it was in trying to make oneself seductive and live in false beauty. Before anyone says, "see it's all demonic", God has no problem in giving His angels, or His bride precious stones.

> *"I will give you hidden treasures, riches stored in secret places, so that you may know that I AM the Lord, the God of Israel, who summons you by name." (Isaiah 45:3)*

> *"I delight greatly in the Lord: my soul rejoices in my God. For He has clothed me with garments of salvation and arrayed me in a robe of His righteousness, as a bridegroom adorns His head like a priest, and as a bride adorns herself with her jewels." (Isaiah 61:10)*

One internet writer, Glenn Pease, concludes that God is the 'Master Jeweller',

> "God was making jewellery of great beauty, with gold and precious stones, before man was ever created. He made Satan a fabulous garment of jewellery when he was created, which was long before man was created. So, the study of jewellery is not only prehistoric, but pre-existence of the universe. In other words, jewels existed in God's realm of existence in eternity before God created what we know as the universe. Jewels are heavenly elements that existed before the universe, and will be a part of heaven when the universe, as we know it, is no more... God was a jeweller before he created our world, and thus, we see from the start, God is a great lover of jewels. This explains why He is so extravagant

with them in the walls of the New Jerusalem... If man can make a model [of jewellery] so beautiful, what will the reality be like, made by the Master Jeweller Himself."[12]

Dr. Eli Lizorkin Eyzenberg says, regarding the white stone Jesus gives overcomers,

> "Receiving 'The Hidden Manna and the White Stone' (Revelation 2:17) – The White Stone was given to overcomers of a trial, as a victory stone, in ancient times (We would say these days by His Grace). A white stone of acquittal (IV Maccabee 15:26; Acts 26:10). Among the most likely interpretations that may fit the context of Revelation 2:17, is a suggestion that the white stones, with names of the recipients inscribed, were given to contest winners (overcomers) of the Roman sport races. The white stone, inscribed with a personal name, presumably served as a pass to a prestigious banquet, only attended by the winners. This stone would have been received upon completion of the race. While this is not a particularly Jewish cultural reference, we do know of many biblical examples of the use of Greco-Roman cultural references as illustrations for and by the Jews. For example, the Apostle Paul used many Roman sports metaphors to make his points (Philippians 3:12-14; 1 Corinthians 9:24-27; 2 Timothy 4:6-8). The writer of the letter of Hebrews also employed Roman sport imagery of running a race and receiving a winner's wreath (See also Hebrews 12:1). This kind of imagery was well known in Judea that housed elaborate sports arenas. This kind of analogy much more closely matches the culture of the Roman city of Pergamum. No doubt the persecuted Believers, both Jewish, and former pagans, were aware of this practice and the elaborate

---

[12] Glenn Pease (2014) *The Jewels of Heaven*. www.sermons.faithlife.com

banquets of honour for the overcomers/winners of the race. Most of the Believers did not take part in the games by virtue of the fact that the games included a dedication to the Roman gods. Christ tells them that in all reality, they have not missed out on anything. The real race and overcomers will receive a pass into the Heavenly banquet of eternal honour."[13]

This white victory stone, given to Believers when they reach Heaven, offers insight to Believers today, who are receiving manifested victory stones after great trials. These stones are a foretaste to the ultimate white stone Believers will receive at the end of the race (Revelation 2:17).

There are also stories from many sources about the Tzohar Stone. They say that when Adam and Eve sinned, a spark of the primordial light of creation was placed into a glowing stone. Some say this stone came from the Pishon river infused with the light of God. When Adam sinned, one story says, he was given a glowing diamond to take with him when he was expelled from the garden. This stone was said to have been passed down through the generations all the way to Noah, and on to Abraham. It is believed that Abraham wore this precious stone around his neck.

This legend is found in the writing of "B. Sanhedrin 108b; Y. Pesahim 1:1; Genesis Rabbah 31:11; Midrash Aggadah; Akedat Yitzak 4; Targum Yonathan on Genesis 16:6, Genesis 8:22; Midrash Aseret Halkhut in Otzar ha-Midrashim, p.444; IFA 4382.[14]

There is another Midrash that says Adam was given a book in the Garden in Eden. And because there was no written parchment, it was engraved on a sapphire stone. As Adam held it up to his

---

13 Dr. Eli Lizorkin Eyzenberg from https://israelbiblicalstudies.com/bible-jewish-studies/#bible-studies

14 Howard Schwartz, Tree of Souls: The mythology of Judaism, Oxford University Press, 2004, p.88.

eyes, a flame burned inside and took the form of the letters, so Adam could read them. The Midrash attempts to explain the verse: "This is the book of the generations of Adam (Genesis 5:1) – (B. Avodah Zarah 5a).[15]

---

15 Schwartz, p. 254.

CHAPTER THREE

They came down from Heaven! Jewish Rabbis

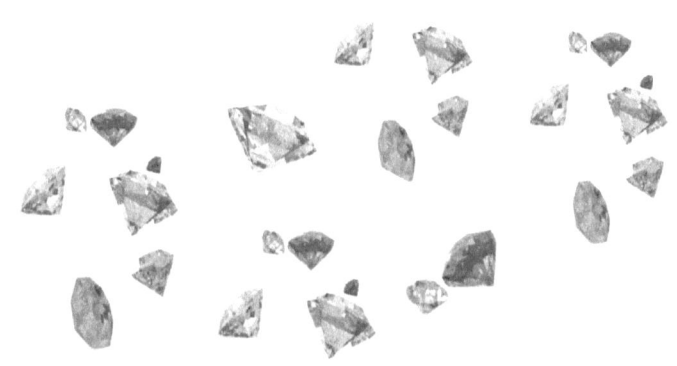

In this Chapter, we will look at one of the most researched books printed on gemstones from a Jewish historical context called *Diamonds and Gemstones in Judaica*. After much searching, I found this rare book on an online second-hand bookshop in England and bought it for its precious insights. In this book, there are a number of references to gemstones coming down from Heaven.

Most quotes come from the work/book, *Diamonds and Gemstones in Judaica*, written by three Professors at the University of Bar'Ilan – Rabbi Zvi Ilani, Rabbi Yitzhak Goldberg, and Rabbi Jaakov Weinberger. They quote from early Jewish writings, which include the Aggadic, including excerpts and commentaries from the Bible, the Midrash, the Mishna, and the Talmud. Also included are quotes from "Our sage of blessed memory."

The purpose of this Chapter is to acknowledge stories and beliefs that precious stones came down from Heaven.

> "Rabbi Bloch recounts a Midrash. The Midrash tells about Rabbi Shimon Ben Hal-Phta who was really impoverished and prayed to God to provide him wealth. A part of a hand came down from the Heavens and gave him a precious stone. Rabbi Shimon sold it and bought provisions for the Sabbath" (Midrash Tehillim 92)[1]

We are not told who's hand it is, but it could be God's or an angel.

The Talmud relates a similar story about Rabbi Hanina Ben Dosa, in which a gold table leg, part of his table in the world to come, was offered to him from Heaven.[2]

---

[1] Rabb Zvi Ilani, Rabbi Yitzhak Goldberg, Rabbi Jaakov Weinberger, *Diamonds and Gemstones in Judaica*, Harry Oppenheimer Diamond Museum, p. 128.
[2] Zvi Ilani, p.129.

> "Rabbi Bloch explains that the physical world is a corridor of the spiritual world which exists above it. The physical man in this world becomes part of the spiritual world in the World to Come. The physical commandments which he fulfilled in this life, become spiritual light in the next world. The Sages echoed this reasoning when they said, "Everything that exists above exists below: above 'Seraphs hover above him: and 'Acacia trees stand (which were used for the building of the tabernacle). Thus, the gem that came down to the physical world can be understood as spiritual in the World to Come. Above, he himself would be glowing, brilliant and valuable: while in this world, he assumed the form of a precious stone – glowing, brilliant and highly valued."[3]

We are told that the gem that came down was representative of a symbolic standing or reward in the world to come.

> "Targum Yonason writes that heavenly clouds brought the stones from the Pishon River (see Bereishis 2:11) to the wilderness, where the heads of the Shevatim found them and donated them to the Mishkan."[4]

The Midrash (Exodus Rabb, chapter 33) indicates another source for the precious stones:

> "Along with the manna which fell for Israel in the desert and provided them with sustenance, precious stones and jewels fell. The leaders of Israel came and gathered them and stored them for the tabernacle."[5]

---

3 Zvi Ilani, p.129.
4 Rabbi Ozer Alport, *Was There Enough – or too much?* (February 2019).
5 Zvi Ilani, p.115.

Again, we see the deep conviction that more was happening in the wilderness than just manna falling. We are told the clouds dropped precious stones and jewels.

> The second gem mentioned in the Talmud is the Margalit. It refers to a precious gem in general (e.g. a jewel). The Latin and Greek translations also understand it as such. This is the meaning of the Midrash which says, "Precious stones and Margaliot fell down for them, for Israel, with the manna" (Yoma 7:5)"[6]

> "The third gem mentioned in the Talmud is the Paz. In the Talmud, there is a story about a ceremony which was held during a Roman festival. During the festival, one person wore a precious gem hung from his neck, which was worth 200 zuzes and called a pizza (Tractate Avodah Zara 12). Rashi emphasizes that 'it is a very precious gem which is not found anywhere in the world." Only two such gems came down to earth, Two stones of Paz which equalled the weight of a stater (a small Persian coin) came down to earth. One is located in Rome, and the other in another place. According to Rashi's testimony, they no longer exist."[7]

> "The ra'mot is mentioned among those stones whose worth is inferior to wisdom (Job 28 28:18). It is also counted among the gems brought to Tyre from Aram (Ezekiel 28:16). Rashi comments that 'these are precious stones from the sea.' The Malbim explains (in reference to the verse in Ezekiel) that these gems suggest superiority and elevation (the word 'rama' in Hebrew means lofty). They are stones which are said to have descended from above."[8]

---

6   Zvi Ilani, p.101.
7   Zvi Ilani, p.102.
8   Zvi Ilani, p.99.

Midrash Rabba, Kohelet, Chapter 10, and Midrash Tanhuma on Exodus, Ki Tetze 27),

> "Where did Moses our teacher's wealth come from? Rabbi Hanin responded: 'From the quarry of sapphire which the Holy One Blessed be He showed him in his tent. And he (Moses) found it, and from that, he became wealthy.' As it is written 'hew yourself two tablets of stone' – the chips shall be for you".[9]

Ancient Jewish scholars state that the sapphire employed for the tables (Ten Commandments), was taken from the throne of glory.

The following quotes refer more to the work and use of precious stones in Heaven, and how the Jews relate the Torah to gemstones.

> "This we learn from Pirkei Hechalot, (Chapter 10) – The ministering angel Darniel came and said to me, 'My dear friend, come, and I shall bring you into the hidden secrets of comfort and salvation'. And I saw groups of ministering angels sitting and weaving clothes of salvation, making crowns of life and setting them with precious stones and pearls, brewing many kinds of perfumes and sweetening wine for the righteous. And I saw one crown, and the sun and the moon and the twelve signs of the Zodiac were set in it. I said to the angel, 'Glorious splendour of the Heavens, what are these crowns for?' He replied, 'For David, the King of Israel.' I said to him, 'Glorious splendour of the Heavens, I see the majesty of David.' He said to me, 'wait a couple of hours, my dear friend, until David, King of Israel comes at the appointed time, and you shall truly see his greatness'."[10]

---

9 Zvi Ilani, p.24.
10 Zvi Ilani, p.132

"This is how the wicked shall also find the righteous on the Judgment day! The Holy One, Blessed be He, says to the people of Israel, 'The wicked shall come and shall see the goodness rewarded the righteous; the people of Israel answer; They shall come and be ashamed, as it is written, 'You shall see my enemy, and you shall be covered with shame.' At this very hour, the wicked come to the entrance of the Garden of Eden, and they stand watching the goodness rewarded to the righteous, and they see all the righteous dressed in royal clothing, with royal crowns set with jewels of pearls fit for kings. And each one sits like a king on a chair of gold, and set before him is a table of pearls. And in each and everyone's hand is a golden cup inlaid with precious stones and pearls, and it is filled with the elixir of life. And all the delicacies of the Garden of Eden are placed before them, and ministering angels stand ready to serve them." (Otzar HaMirashim)[11]

"The World to Come is also the world of eternal rewards and is paved with precious stones. In the World to Come, the Holy One, Blessed be He, shall sit on His throne of Justice and shall call each and every righteous man by name, and shall give each and every one a good reward for his deeds... and He shall build him, (each) righteous man, two palaces made of nofech, sapir and yahalom, and each gem shall be 765 cubits by four cubits." (Batai Midrashot, Part 2, Midrash Alpha Beta)[12]

"So said Elijah the prophet, 'I see the houses and gates of the righteous, their doorposts are made of precious stones, and the treasures of the temple are open to their doors, and between these are Torah and peace.' This is not to mention the portion of the Messiah, the

---

11 Zvi Ilani, p.133
12 Zvi Ilani, p.133

King himself, The Holy One, Blessed be He, shall make for the Messiah seven canopies of precious stones and pearls...and He shall embrace him in front of the righteous and shall lead him to the canopy." (Persikita Rabbati, Chapter 38).[13]

"You shall hoard my commandments; you shall guard My Torah like a person who owns a jewel." (Tanhuma, Ekev 5)[14]

In the Midrash on the Song of Songs (song of song Rabba 2) – we meet a mature and evenly balanced son, whose father merely waits for the son to assert his claim. "There was a king who owned a precious stone and jewels. His son approached him and said, 'Give it to me.' The king replied, 'They are yours, all yours, and I am giving them to you.' 'This is for Israel', said the Holy One, Blessed be He, as it is written, 'the Lord is my strength and song.' The Holy One, blessed be He, said to them: 'This is yours, all yours and I am giving it to you.' As it is written, 'the Lord gives strength.' And that is no strength other than Torah".[15]

In this Chapter and the Chapter before we have seen that it is a held belief by the Jews and their Rabbis that

1. Gemstones are in Heaven.
2. Gemstones came down from Heaven in the wilderness with the manna.
3. Moses got his first two tablet stones from Heaven.
4. The Urim & Thummim stones that fitted in the Priests pouch were said to not be from this world, but from above.
5. Some gemstones originated in Heaven and were very rare on earth.

---

13 Zvi Ilani, p.133
14 Zvi Ilani, p.82
15 Jacob Neusner, *A Theological Commentary to the Midrash: Song of Song Rabbat*, UPA, 2001, p.85

6. Angels brought gemstones down to earth and even gave rings with precious stones in.
7. Stories exist of gemstones coming down from Heaven from a miraculous hand.
8. Gemstones are rewards in Heaven for the world to come.

CHAPTER FOUR

Controversy, Glassy, Plastic, Fake – Not so Fast!

When it comes to the stones manifesting, I am not one to shy away from so-called controversy. In this Chapter, I will address this issue and hope it gives understanding and correction. The phenomenon of gemstones appearing from Heaven is happening all around the world in churches, houses, parks, you name it. As I have studied this phenomenon for the last six years, I have corresponded with others who have experienced these manifestations around the world, to ask questions and confirmations.

A number of years ago, stones were appearing in an area where I was staying. I saw these stones appear out of thin air. There was much excitement and wonder, as it was indeed a miracle before the eyes. But many of these stones looked just glassy, or even to some, plastic. To this much criticism came. Some were immediately taken to jewellers to find out what they were, or even for an evaluation (wrong motive). When they were told they were just glass, people started to reject them. Some stones, because they looked clear or plastic, were called fake. Now I have seen glassy stones appear, and I have seen solid gems appear, even clasped with a gold casing. On one occasion, I even saw a young child, while in vision, bring down a chunk of Greenstone as a gift for a Maori Church. All of them supernaturally appeared. One time, 250 appeared at one church.

The questions we need to ask and reflect on, are, "does the material they appear in determine if they are real (true) or fake?" "Is God's only purpose to give valuable stones to all people?"

Does the Bible not warn us, *"God does not judge outwards appearances, but sees the heart"*? (1 Samuel 16:7)

Well, in my research and dialogs with people who have received thousands of stones over the years, some being 50 Carat to 1000 Carat gemstones, of which many have been tested by gemmologists to be real (and worth a lot), they do record that at times, or in the beginning, they too, had these small, glassy, plastic (no one knows the material) stones appearing.

These people have had diamonds, and all sorts of precious stones turn up. So, it shows we must not be too quick to judge or ridicule God. He has many purposes, and He does not just entrust diamonds or rubies into anyone's hands. Can you be trusted? Do you have faith? What does your heart reflect, and what do you carry in the spirit? All is resembled in the stones.

The stones are gifts, and many do carry a weight of glory on them. Jeff Jansen has had stones appear in meetings, that have been tested, and are cut so perfect they are believed to not be of this world (50 Carat Rubies).

In dialogue with Dr. Glenn Smith, who has written a great book called, *Gemstones from Heaven* and has received thousands of stones (solid 50 -1000 Carat stones) over the years from Heaven, shared an experience he had with me which I found enlightening:

> "I once was at a friend's house and found a plastic stone, obviously like the child's necklace that broke. I didn't choose to believe that God would put something meaningless in my path, so I took a picture and enlarged it. Everyone said I would not see anything. I found Hebrew writing inside it. God will and can give us what He wants and when He wants. It is up to us to choose faith."

I also have a friend who received a stone from Heaven, who took it to a jeweller to have it placed in a ring. The jeweller was shocked when he put it under the microscope and saw Hebrew writing in the stone. He said, "Where did you get this stone from, and how did the writing get inside?", which he said was impossible. The words in the stone in Hebrew spelt the nickname her husband used to call her. God likes the fine details.

I can remember going to Germany with a few of my stones on me. These were glassy ones, and at this large conference, I pulled them out to show two Pastors. The stones in my hand came alive, pulsating with presence. As one of the Pastors put his hand over my hand, he was slain on the floor by the presence of God on the stones. They are real, not fake – don't be too quick to rubbish the simple things or those things that can confound the wise.

In another dialogue with a man called Michael C. King, who also has a great book called, *Gemstones from Heaven*, and has had thousands of solid stones appear of all types, recounts one time he saw stones appear and they looked plastic/glassy:

> "Shortly thereafter, I was walking to the food table and saw a gem sparkle on the ground. I picked it up, quite excited, and showed the friends and my wife. I walked back towards the food table and found another one. My wife directed me to look under the chairs next to me, and there were almost a dozen more beneath this row of chairs. I quickly picked them up, delighted. After all, what were the chances? Fast forward an hour later, and I realized that these gems appeared to be low quality and were actually lighter than the gems I was used to feeling. Turns out they were plastic. I cannot help that God chooses to do things that confound me. Why not real gems? I have no idea."[1]

Michael says in his book, speaking of solid gemstones:

> "Sometimes the gems will grow in size, they can be prayed for when chipped, and heal, even multiply. One of our grandchildren put one in a box once, and when she opened the box again, a second smaller one, that was otherwise identical, was sitting next to it. The gem had a baby."[2]

---

1   Michael C. King, *Gemstones from Heaven*, self-published, 2016, p.37
2   King, p.10

Michael shares the experience of a friend,

> "We have had gems tested, and when different people brought the same gem into the same jeweller, he got different results based on what the person who brought the stone believed about the stone."[3]

I have seen stones change colour, and my friend Jason Cobb has seen stones heal up.

Dr. Glenn Smith gives a couple of accounts of seeing gemstones grow in size, for they are living stones:

> "God brought me to a Denny's restaurant with a group of people. Four gems fell on the table, these were diamond-looking gems that God had sent to so many places... I picked them up, and they started to grow in my hand. The entire restaurant was looking at it. The manager and waitress of the restaurant watched this happen, and after dinner, we started to depart."[4]

> "I was speaking at a conference with a few hundred people. God spoke to me to do a couple of things...We had about 30 gems put into people's hands and then said, "watch them grow". THEY GREW. When the gems grew, it was like an explosion of faith. When people see the gems grow while they hold them, or when people around them say, 'grow'; it is amazing, because the growth testifies to the power of God and the knowledge that these are, in fact, living stones".[5]

Michael C. King reports on some stones appearing in settings and even a pendant,

---

3   King, p.24
4   Glenn & Terrie Smith, *Gemstones from Heaven*, Netturtle Studios, 2014, p.223
5   Smith, p. 225

"Rarer still, probably close to one in five thousand gems or more, will be a stone that appears in a setting of some kind. This can be a ring, cuff links, pendant, or earrings. On at least one occasion that I know of, the chain even appeared with the pendant."[6]

This reminds me of Ezekiel 16:11-14:

"I adorned you with jewellery: I put bracelets on your arms and a necklace around your neck, and I put a ring on your nose, earrings on your ears and a beautiful crown on your head. So you were adorned with gold and silver: your clothes were of fine linen and costly fabric and embroidered cloth. Your food was honey, olive oil, and the finest flour. You became very beautiful and rose to be a queen. And your fame spread among the nations on account of your beauty, because the splendour I had given you made your beauty perfect, declares the Sovereign Lord."

In fact, I even know of people who are receiving precious stones mounted in rings. This manifestation most likely connects with the Parable of the Lost Son receiving a ring (Luke 15:21-22). A signet ring in Scripture, many times speaks of a transfer of authority.

Many people around the world are receiving precious stones and very valuable stones. But I believe these stones come with a cost, for where your heart is, so also is your treasure. There can be stones that are gifts from God, and there can be stones that speak of functions in the kingdom. A priest, a bride, and a king have different functions, and each carries a weight of glory in adorning stones. And sometimes God just gives expensive gifts.

Many of the stones that appear are not of great earthly value, some are semi-precious. Many just look like glassy stones. Scripture calls these "glistening stones" (1 Chronicles 29:2). And no, they

---

6 King, p.10

weren't bought from China or some online-shop. These small glass stones I have seen, change colour and grow in size and pulsate with presence. Isaiah 54:11-12 describes our foundations and walls as being adorned with "colourful gems" and precious stones. So, we have different grades of stones in Scripture, colourful gems, glistening stones, and precious stones.

It is evident from the above accounts that these stones are not fake. They are real, and they have appeared before people's eyes miraculously, including my own.

In the last four Chapters, we have analysed and concluded:

1. Gemstones are manifesting today like in the wilderness,
2. The idea of manifesting gemstones in Biblical times is held by Jewish authorities & Biblical Scholars,
3. When controversy appears, we must check our assumptions and definitions carefully with other certified experiences.

In the following Chapters, I will attempt to lay a Biblical foundation from the Scriptures, on what the Bible is saying about gemstones and why Scripture would hint that they would manifest again in our age.

CHAPTER FIVE

The Creation Covenant

> *For God so loved the cosmos, that He gave His one and only Son. (John 3:16)*

This well-known verse means much more than just betrothing humanity. God was in Christ betrothing creation to be His bride. God's bride is multi-dimensional and fills creation.

> *"The earth is the Lords, and its fullness, the world and those who dwell therein. For He has founded it upon the seas and established it upon the waters. Who may ascend into the hill of the Lord, or who may stand in His holy place." (Psalm 24:1-4)*

> *"For the Lord will comfort Zion, He will comfort all her waste places, He will make her wilderness like Eden, and her desert like the garden of the Lord." (Isaiah 51:3)*

Dinah Dye, in her book The Temple Revealed In The Garden, says:

> "In the beginning, God cut a covenant with Heaven and Earth and bound them together in marriage. The Heavens represented the bridegroom and the Earth the bride. Their union formed God's Cosmic House, and from the womb of the earth (ancient cultures believed the womb equalled a sanctuary) the seed of creation sprouted."[1]

We can see right from the beginning that God made a "creation covenant" with creation, bringing her into being, to be His bride. When Dye speaks of the seed of creation, she is talking about Adam coming out of the dust.

---

1 Dinah Dye, *The Temple Revealed in The Garden: Priests and Kings*. Foundations in Torah Publishers, 2015, p.71

Dinah Dye, in her book The Temple Revealed in Creation, says:

> "The sages (Jewish Rabbis) believed that, "In the beginning, before creation, the world was but water in water" (Genesis Rabbah 5:2). Then, God separated the waters. The male waters above were divided from the female waters below: the female waters were called tehom (deep)…Rabbi Abahu referred to the upper waters as a bridegroom and the lower waters as a bride…Creation could be defined, then, as the reuniting of male and female elements in order for two to become one house and to produce life. The Creation Covenant is essentially a covenant related to betrothal and marriage. This is temple-building activity, for to build a temple was to build a house and family."[2]

Dye goes on to say,

> "The Creation Covenant is not specifically named in the Bible: it is hidden in the Hebrew letters of the first word, Beresheet: in the beginning. Two Hebrew words from the word Beresheet: brit, meaning "covenant," and esh, meaning "fire". The Creation Covenant was the Covenant of fire…Although brit is translated "to cut", it really means 'joining" together two halves. A covenant, therefore, describes a relationship in which two join together to become one. A marriage covenant is an example of the "covenant of fire."[3]

M. Barker says,

> "The biblical worldview is a vision of the unity of all things, and how the visible material world relates to

---

[2] Dinah Dye, *The Temple Revealed in Creation: A Portrait of The Family*. Foundations in Torah Publishers, 2016, p.17

[3] Dye, p.21

another dimension of existence that unites all things into one divinely ordained system known as the eternal covenant, the Creation Covenant."[4]

We actually see this covenant in Hosea 2:20-23:

> *"When the day comes, I will make a covenant for them with the wild animals, the birds in the air and the creeping things of the earth. I will break bow and sword, sweep battle from the land and make them lie down securely. I will betroth you to me forever: yes, I will betroth you to me in righteousness, in justice, in grace, and in compassion: I will betroth you to me in faithfulness, and you will know the Lord. When that day comes, I will answer, says the Lord I will answer the sky and it will answer the earth."*

In the Chapters to follow, I will be presenting many reasons and functions for why gemstones are manifesting today. I will present a strong case for the adorning of the priest, bride, and kingly functions. But if I was to give just one argument for why gemstones are manifesting today, I could make the case, that if God adorns His bride with jewels and creation is His bride, then gemstones can manifest anywhere, anytime in creation. For creation is the Cosmic house/temple of God, the Bride.

> *"For He has clothed me with the garments of salvation, He has covered me with the robe of righteousness, as a bridegroom decks himself with ornaments, and the bride adorns herself with her jewels."* (Isaiah 61:10)

---

4 M.Baker, *Creation: A Biblical Vision for the Environment*, London, T&T Clark, 2010, p.19

God has decked Himself with ornaments in Heaven, precious stones are everywhere. And He can adorn His many multi-dimensional brides with jewels.

> *"Through wisdom, a house is built, and by understanding, it is established. By knowledge, the rooms are filled with precious and pleasant riches." (Proverbs 24:3-4)*

If creation is God's house, His bride, then He can fill its rooms and adorn His rooms with jewels to show forth beauty and glory. And these rooms can be in fields, parks, gardens, houses, churches, and basically anywhere in creation. If creation is a house, a bride, then anywhere on or in the house (bride, creation) precious stones can appear.

> *"That in the dispensation of the fullness of the times He might gather together in one all things in Christ, both which are in Heaven and which are on earth - in Him." (Ephesians 1:10)*

CHAPTER SIX

The Priest Adorned with Jewels

The Priest was one authorised to perform the sacred rites in the Tabernacle and be the mediator between man and God. In 1 Peter 2:5 it says that all Believers in Christ are priests in the royal priesthood. "You also as living stones are being built up a spiritual house, a holy priesthood to offer up spiritual sacrifices…".

As a priest of God, we are to be adorned with precious jewels. One of the aspects of the stones on the priest's robe was the function of reflecting divine Heavenly glory. God commands Moses to make *"holy garments for Aaron…for glory and for beauty."* (Exodus 28:2)

The word for glory - *Kabod* is the Hebrew word for God's glorious, theophanic revelation of Himself to Israel. The precious stones manifesting today, speak theophanic revelation and beautify us as priests.

Both Josephus and Philo understood the jewels on the priest's breastplate to be symbolic of the twelve constellations, as well as the twelve tribes of Israel. The stones lit up and directed the seasons of the twelve tribes of Israel. As the priest placed the Urim and Thummim stones into his pouch in the Ephod breastplate, they would come alive and shine through the twelve stones and give divine directions of God's will. The Jews have a tradition that the Urim and Thummim stones were not from this world, they were the handiwork of Heaven.

Leslie Hardinge, in his book *Stones of Fire,* says:

> "Josephus thought the twelve precious stones of the breastplate constituted the Urim and Thummim, and that upon these gems the names of the tribes were inscribed. He believed that when they were consulted, particular

letters shone forth from them, spelling out God's message."[1]

But many think this was not the case, it was more the shining of lights and colours.

The twelve stones on the breastplate represented the children of God. The stones were receiving the divine nature of God's will infused into them symbolically, but also in a living way. The stones, from the infusion of God's presence, held a frequency and record in them of the journey of God's people. The stones spoke of their functions and achievements.

> *"Aaron shall bear the names of the children of Israel in the breastplate of judgement upon his heart, when he goeth into the Holy Place, for a memorial before the Lord continually."* (Exodus 28:29)

Hardinge goes on to say:

> "These revelations of God's will were not to any one individual. They were national and also universal in their full application, and God's Word was given to the commonality of mankind. There was no possibility for one here and one there to obtain a different message, or a different set of rules to regulate his conduct. All men were regarded as upon the same base."[2]

This is true today as individual priests, the stones that are manifesting and are related to priest adorning stones, they are speaking about our lives and functions as one body in Christ. And in the Spirit, they speak forth to the whole body of Christ a unifying message, for we are all part of the one spiritual temple (Ephesians 2:21). It is God who fashions them with a revelation for us to

---

[1] Leslie Hardinge, *The Stones of Fire*, American Christian Ministries, 2011, p.7
[2] Hardinge, p.17

steward and become. But they are also a witness, a representation in stone, to those in spirit, to see what we carry in the Kingdom.

The main difference between the priests of old and today, is that we are all priests that intercede, so the stones speak of us individually and corporately.

The setting up of the priesthood is described in great detail in the book of Leviticus which mean's "joined together or united". We see this today in the outworking of the spiritual temple, as priests in the spirit, being fitted together as one. (Ephesians 2:20-22)

Linda Cruz in her book *All His Jewels* says,

> "On the front of the ephod, the breastplate of judgment was fastened to the stones on the shoulders by two chains of pure gold. The breast piece was constructed of gold with one precious jewel for each of the twelve tribes: each engraved with one of their names. The stones were set in four rows of three stones each in the following order: ruby, topaz, emerald, turquoise, sapphire, diamond, jacinth, agate, amethyst, beryl, onyx, and jasper. This breast piece of judgment was worn by the High Priest over his heart at all times as a "memorial" unto the Lord. As the jewels radiated with all colours of the rainbow, God was reminded of His special people, His eternal jewels, who would shine with His glory forever and ever."[3]

As Christ lives in us and shines through us like the Urim and Thummim that was in the high priest's pouch. We are now walking, "Living Stones," shining with the light of God inside us, as the Spirit directs and leads our lives. As a priest today, the manifesting precious stones speak revelation about us. They change colour

---

3   Linda Cruz, *All His Jewels: From Glory to Glory*, Xulon Press, 2007, p. 119

according to seasons, they grow as we mature, they heal when damaged, and they reveal graces on our lives, and they adorn us, for they are living stones reflecting beauty and glory. They are, in a sense, memorial stones.

The stones on the priest's breastplate spoke of God's theophanic revelation and beauty.

- ❖ The stones represented the twelve tribes of Israel.
- ❖ The stones instructed them and taught them revelation.
- ❖ The stones were a symbolic living stone that represented the children of God.
- ❖ As the Priest's garments represented the cosmos, the stones were shown to exist in the Heavenly realms.
- ❖ The stones were a representation of us and a foretaste of future fulfilments.
- ❖ The stones spoke of us going from glory to glory.
- ❖ The stones on the breastplate showed the existence of all the children of God being represented here on earth and in Heaven.
- ❖ The stones also represented the twelve signs of the zodiac, speaking of the children of God's seasons and their victories.
- ❖ The stones held the record of what the priest bared upon his heart for God. For where your heart is, your treasure is also.

The stones on the priest's breastplate resembled many functions, including the twelve tribes of Israel, the children of God, the twelve constellation signs, speaking of our seasons in God, and they spoke of our functions/callings in the Kingdom.

The priest's garments represented the cosmos and the Heavenly realms. As the priest walked and interceded, his 'works' were seen through the 'will' of God shining through the breastplate stones. They held a record of the work that had been accomplished in the Heavens.

As priests walking in our duties, we are adorned with stones of intersession; as brides, we are adorned with stones of love, engagement, and gifts; as kings, we are adorned with stones of power, authority and victories. There are different adornings for different functions.

As we walk on earth interceding (building stones in Heavenly places), the stones are a memorial of our functions, graces, rewards, and gifts. In our priest, bride, and kingly functions, there are degrees of glory, and this is reflected in the stones. For our works will be tested, like gold, silver and precious stones. To him, who is given much, much is required.

G.K Beale says in his book, *The Temple and the Church's Mission*:

> "It is apparent that aspects of the priest's robe contained cosmic symbolism. Like the tabernacle curtains, the various parts of the high priest attire were also woven of 'blue and purple and scarlet material' because it was to reflect the cosmos.
>
> "The jewels on the priest's breast piece were a small replica of the holy of holies, symbolizing the earthly or Heavenly cosmos, and the same jewels are part of the new city-temple in Revelation 21. Both the priest and the tabernacle were designed to represent the creative work of God."[4]

The priest's garment resembles the three sections of the temple. The first the outermost part at the bottom (the outer-court) on which were sewn pomegranates of blue and purple and scarlet along with variegated flowers which represented the fertile earth. Secondly, the main body of the bluish robe (the holy place), within which and on the upper part of which are set the jewels, symbolized the stars that are set in the sky. Thirdly, the square Ephod resembles

---

4   G.K.Beale, *The Temple and the Churches Mission*, InterVarsity Press, 2004, p.39

the square holy of holies, within which were placed the Urim and Thummim, stones representing God's revelatory presence (Glory).[5]

> "The precious stones on the priest's breast correspond partly to the lamps on the lampstand, which connect both to the Heavenly luminaries since both speak of Heavenly stars. The same precious stones and metals are used in the construction of the temple, which are also in the fashioning of the priests clothing. The same precious stones are used to describe the Heavenly dwelling of God, further associating the same stones of the temple and of the priestly raiment with the Heavenly sphere."[6]

Beale shows some of the connections:

> "Sapphire as part of the Heavenly temple (Exodus 24:10; Ezekiel 1:26; 10:1; Revelation21:19), is likely included in the earthly temple (1 Chronicles 29:2), and a facet of the priest's clothing (Exodus 28:18; 39:11); Onyx, as part of the priestly clothing (Exodus 25:7; 28:9, 20; 35:9, 27; 39:6, 13) and of the temple (1 Chronicles 29:2), though not mentioned explicitly in the Heavenly visions; Jasper as part of the priest's attire (Exodus 28:20; 39:13) and of the appearance of the Heavenly temple (Revelation 4:3: 21:11: 18-19), the latter of which also suggest that Jasper was inclined among the precious stones of Solomon's temple; 'Beryl' as part of the priestly apparel (Exodus 28:20: 39:13) and of the structure of the Heavenly temple (Ezekiel 1:16: Revelation 21:20: Daniel 10:6)."[7]

---

5   Beale, p.40
6   Beale, p.40
7   Beale, p.41

"Likewise, both Josephus and Philo understood the garments of the high priest to symbolize the whole cosmos (Philo, Vit. Mos, 2.117-126, 133-135, 143: Josephus, Ant. 3.180, 183-187). Other sectors of Judaism held virtually the same view of the priest's clothing. Wisdom of Solomon 18:24 (2nd century BC – 1st century AD), likewise understands the high priest's garments and jewels to be symbolic of the entire cosmos, in the long garment was the whole world, and in the four rows of the stones was the glory of the Father's."[8]

Hardinge says,

"Jesus shone the Divine Presence of light through the diamond stones on the breastplate, called Urim and Thummim, before His incarnation. Diamond is carbon that has once been part of living cells upon the earth. It points to Jesus, the real Urim and Thummim, who in the very presence of God, stands possessed of human flesh and blood. The incarnation is called Heaven's sign, the true precious stones from above, the Rock. As the diamond Urim and Thummim break up the light of God's will to suit the needs of His people, so the pattern of the precious stones, Christ Himself, is the prism through which the light of the glory of God is revealed to meet our differing requirements. Peter records the fact that there are manifold temptations (1 Peter 1:6). The manifold literally means 'many-coloured'. We use colours to indicate weakness. The apostle further places on record, the divine provision for countering man's manifold temptations. God grace is manifold, or 'many-coloured'. The many-coloured grace of God will

---

8 Beale, p.41

neutralize every sort and shade of trial and weakness, for His grace is sufficient for us Living Stones."[9]

The coloured stones that are manifesting today, speak of the graces and gifts of empowerment that are on our lives.

My friend Jason Cobb has seen damaged gemstones, which came from Heaven, heal up before his eyes. This is due many times to coming through another dimension, but not always.

Michael C. King who has received many perfect stones from Heaven says in his book *Gemstones from Heaven*,

"It seems completely absurd to me, that God would send us gems from Heaven that are flawed, but then aren't we all cracked or blemished in some way? Doesn't God send us as untarnished spirits into the earth, where we then pick up cracks and chips on our journey through life? People have actually prayed for "injured" gems, and they have recovered."[10]

These are all different stories, but as priests, our stones speak about us and give off revelation of glory. The priest's stones we will re-visit in a later Chapter because they go into multi-dimensional layers of revelation. But for our purpose in this Chapter, we have seen that the priest's adorning stones were for revelation and beauty. And as priests, we should expect to receive a covering of adorning stones.

---

9 Hardinge, p.20
10 King, p.26

CHAPTER SEVEN

The Bride Adorned with Her Jewels

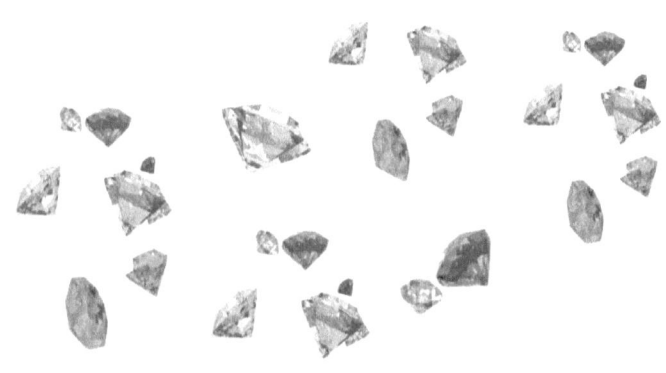

In ancient Jewish culture, the father of the groom was the one who decided whether the groom was ready to marry his betrothed or not. Once the bridegroom's father felt the groom had sufficiently prepared a place for her, the groom would then go and bring his bride to be with him there.

Jesus said in John 14:1-4,

> *"Let not your heart be troubled, you believe in God, believe in Me. In My Father's house are many rooms, if it were not so, I would have told you. I go to prepare a place for you. And if I go and prepare a place for you, I will come again and receive you to Myself, that where I am, there you may be also. And where I go, you know, and the way you know."*

Jesus was making it clear as the bridegroom that it was time for him to go and prepare a room for his bride in his Father's house.

In ancient Jewish culture,

- ❖ When they became betrothed, a gold coin or jewels were given, and as the bridegroom went away for twelve months, the jewels were a reminder of his love. (Genesis 24:53)
- ❖ If we spiritualise the Jewish culture, the father of the groom is God (Father), and the bridegroom is Jesus. The Father chose us (all Believers) to marry Jesus. Therefore, Jesus as the bridegroom goes away to prepare a place for us, the bride.
- ❖ When the bridegroom came to collect his bride, he would adorn her with jewels then take her to his father's house to be with him forever. The bridegroom collecting his bride is Jesus leading us through life, our wilderness, and bringing us to the Father's house in Heaven (as a married couple). And it is along this journey, that we are adorned with jewels.
- ❖ They say that, in the wilderness, "precious stones fell with the manna." God was leading, comforting and encouraging His people, His bride to walk with Him.

- ❖ Through life, in wilderness seasons, in the waiting for the bridegroom, God leads and comforts and adorns us. And in this season, it is with precious stones from above, that He is gifting us. Many of the stones, manifesting today, are love stones.
- ❖ *"I will greatly rejoice in the Lord, my soul shall be joyful in my God: For He has clothed me with the garments of salvation, He has covered me with the robe of righteousness, as a bridegroom decks himself with ornaments, and as a bride adorns herself with her jewels."* (Isaiah 61:10)
- ❖ On our way to the Father's House, on the journey, we must not forget our bridegroom (Jesus), for He has always shown covenant with engagement and love.
- ❖ *"O generation, see the word of the Lord! Have I been a wilderness to Israel, or a land of darkness? Why do My people say, we are lords, we will come no more to You? Can a virgin forget her ornaments, or a bride her attire? Yet My people have forgotten Me days without number."* (Jeremiah 2:31-32)

Jewels speak of intimacy with God. If God adorns his people, why are so many today rejecting His manifesting gifts, and forgetting His love? God wants to adorn His bride. and those who open their hearts, He will adorn with jewels.

Brant Pitre, in his book *Jesus the Bridegroom,* says:

> "Perhaps the most powerful of all these images of the new Israel is John's description of the bride of Jesus, as being adorned with twelve kinds of jewels: jasper, sapphire, agate, and so on (Revelation 21:19-20). As any first century Jew would have recognized, this is not just a random set of jewels. The bride of Jesus is covered with the twelve jewels worn by the Jewish high priest when

offering sacrifice in the Tabernacle; jewels symbolizing the twelve tribes of Israel."[1]

One thing we must take note of is the bride was not only adorned with those twelve stones. A bride's adornment was of the highest value a family could afford and was typically provided to her by her betrothed husband in the form of a dowry or gifts. The headpiece alone could weigh several kilograms. Rings, gold coins, nose jewels, and necklaces with strings of jewels were given. A diadem or draped, forehead jewel was also worn as a headdress. All of these would need many precious stones.

Single and the collective bride - In Christ, we are described as being Christ's bride. This is spoken of individuals and as a collective bride – the Church. As individuals (bride), this is why there are many rooms in the Father's House (John 14:2-3). And the bride is also known as being collectively one, as the Church, the body of Christ, and the city in Heaven.

When it comes to the phenomena of God adorning His bride on her way (the journey of life) to the Father's House (Heaven), there is one truth that must be understood very clearly. Many people all around the world are receiving stones from above, and it's easy for those who are not, to feel left out, or inferior, or even condemned with the "Who has", and the "Who has not". The truth is, there are no favourites or super saints, but there are some truths one must recognize concerning the stones manifesting.

- ❖ The stones are a reminder to all, that He (God) is pursuing His bride with love (Jeremiah 2:32).
- ❖ The stones are a sign and a wonder – a mystery full of love revelations.
- ❖ God distributes to each one as He wills (1 Corinthians 12:6, 2:11).

---

1 Brant Pitre, *Jesus the Bridegroom: The Greatest Love Story Ever Told*, Crown Publishing, p.126

- ❖ A stone is a taste of the substance of faith, it is not a physical requirement.
- ❖ Yes, different stones can carry different meanings and functions. Many stones carry different weights of glory and preciousness, but it is the Lord's doing. Most stones are gift stones when it comes to the bride's adorning.
- ❖ There are many types of stones, and not all are precious, and they all have different functions. There are precious stones, glistening stones and coloured stones (1 Chronicles 29:2). Don't judge them as true or false (fake) based on how expensive the stones are.
- ❖ There are different stones for the adorning of priest, king, and bride.
- ❖ All Believers whether they receive a stone on earth or not – will have their adorning stones in Heaven. Victory stones, gift stones, adorning stones, function stones, and authority stones.
- ❖ As with all gifts, we can engage God and ask for any gift.
- ❖ Just as an individual can receive a stone, so can a stone manifest in a church service and be for the whole church, adorning the collective bride.
- ❖ Any stone, manifested in a gathering, can be for the spiritual body worldwide collectively – You included. The Bride is the Bride.
- ❖ Some stones come with angels that stay for a season, and after the season, these stones may disappear. Seasonal love gifts…
- ❖ God engaged His people in the wilderness, with love, gifts, and encouragement. He rained down manna and precious stones. It was a sign, a wonder, but not every person in Israel got one. They understood them as God's hand upon them as a whole nation, a people.
- ❖ Just because you or I haven't received manna like in the wilderness, or food multiplying, or a coin in a fish's mouth, it does not make us inferior. Therefore, we should celebrate the gifts of others as they speak of us, too.

Ian Clayton in his book "Realms of the Kingdom, Volume Two", says,

> "When the son or daughter of a Hebrew family married a Gentile, after the bride and bridegroom had come out of the huppah, they would take diamond, gold and sapphire dust and throw it over the bride and bridegroom as the power of endowment and their acceptance and sanctification of marriage. Did you wonder why gold, diamonds, sapphires and precious stones are showing up?"[2]

Howard Schwarz, in his book, *Tree of Souls: The Mythology of Judaism,* reveals deeper insights about the adorning of stones, that they are part of the wedding canopy over the bride:

> "When they are first engaged, God sends His betrothed nuptial presents and a meal of celestial bread. So, too, does He make preparations for the wedding feast. On the eve of Shavuot, before the wedding takes place, the members of the Heavenly household remain with the Bride all night, and rejoice in the preparations for the wedding… Throughout the night, the Bride rejoices with Her maidens and is made ready by them. And in the morning, she enters the bridal canopy, illumined with the radiance of sapphire, which shines from one end of the world to the other…On Friday, the six of Sivan, the day appointed by the Lord for the revelation of the Torah to His beloved people, God came forth from Mount Sinai. The Groom, the Lord, the King of Hosts, is betrothed to the bride, the community of Israel, arrayed in beauty. The Bridegroom said to the pious and virtuous maiden, Israel, who had won His favour above all others, 'Can there be a bridal canopy without a bride? As I live' – declares the Lord – 'you shall

---

2   Ian Clayton, *Realms of the Kingdom*. Sons of Thunder Publications, 2016, p. 75

don them all like jewels, deck yourself with them like a bride. Many days will you be Mine, and I will be your Redeemer'."[3]

As we can see, God gives adorning gifts for the Bride to wear and also covers the wedding canopy (Huppah) with Sapphire and precious stones. The Jewish Rabbis even believe that Eve was adorned with precious stones as the example of the first wedding of creation.

Howard Schwartz writes further:

> "When Adam awoke and saw Eve standing in front of him, their faces illuminating each other, he understood at once that he had found his true mate. God introduced Adam to Eve and explained how she had been created. Then Adam embraced her and kissed her and said, "This one, at last, is bone of my bones and flesh of my flesh. This one shall be called Woman, for from man was she taken." (Gen 2:23). Then God knew that the time had come for the world's first wedding. God Himself prepared tables of precious pearls and filled them with delicacies. God also created ten wedding canopies for them, all made of precious stones, pearls and gold. So too did he attire Eve, the first bride, in a beautiful wedding dress, and braid her hair and adorn her with twenty-four different ornaments.
>
> Sources: B. Eruvin 18a: B. Berakhot 61a: B. Niddah 45a: B. Shabbat 95a: Genesis Rabbah 8:13, 18:1: Pesikta de-Rav Kahana 4:4, 26:3: Pirkei de-Rabbi Eliezer 12: Avot de-Rabbi Natan 4: Sefer ha – Zikhronot 7:1-2: Pesikta Rabbati 14:10: Zohar 3:19a, 3:44b."[4]

---

[3] Howard Schwartz. *Tree of Souls: Mythology of Judaism*, Oxford Press, 2004, p.304 -305

[4] Schwartz, p.143

It is interesting to note that the twenty-four ornaments, of which they say Eve was covered, they draw from Isaiah 3:17-23,

> *"The jingling anklets, the scarves, and the crescents, the pendants, the bracelets, and the veils, the headdresses, the leg ornaments, and the headbands, the perfume boxes, the charms, and the rings, the nose jewels, the festal apparel, and the mantles, the outer garments, the purses, and the mirrors, the fine linen, the turbans, and the robes."*

Adam and Eve wore robes of light, reflecting the light of God's glory. But when they sinned their eyes *"were opened, and they knew that they were naked, and they sewed fig leaves together and made themselves aprons."* (Genesis 3:7) The glory and their spiritual covering lifted.

> *"I exalt in the Lord, my soul rejoices in my God, for he has wrapped me in the cloak of integrity, like a bridegroom wearing his wreath, like a bride adorned in her jewels."* (Isaiah 61:10)

Jesus spoke about the wedding garments of the kingdom, the spiritual clothing!

Let us wonder at the sign and fall in love with our Bridegroom.

CHAPTER EIGHT

Not just a Priest, a Bride, but also a King!

> *"And [He] has made us Kings and Priests to His God and Father, to Him be glory and dominion forever and ever."* (Revelation 1:6)

As a priest, we are adorned with jewels; as the bride, we are adorned with jewels; and also, as a king, we are adorned with jewels.

It seems we will be covered with many jewels, of different functions and authority and size.

A king was showered with precious stones in his kingdom. The Queen of Sheba came to see King Solomon and brought him precious stones.

> *"She came to Jerusalem with a very great retinue, with camels that bore spices, very much gold, and precious stones, and when she came to Solomon, she spoke with him all that was in her heart."* (1 Kings 10:2)

When a king wished to repay a great favour to a person who had greatly aided him, he would bestow on him a gift of precious stones (Tractate Taanit 21). As Jesus is the King of kings, and we are kings, his favour can be adorned on us as of precious stones.

In the Book *Diamonds and Gemstones in Judaica*, authored by Rabbi Zvl Ilanl, Rabbi Yitzhak Goldberg, and Rabbi Jaakov Weinberger, it states,

> "Sometimes stones were removed from their hiding places and coffers. When a king wished to shower another king with gifts, he would send him precious stones."

Isaiah 45:3 says that the King of kings will give hidden treasures from secret places:

> *"I will give you the treasures of darkness, and hidden riches of secret places, that you may know that I the Lord, Who called you by your name, I Am the God of Israel."*

The wealth of the kingdom is like authority and spiritual power we carry as kings. We are adorned with jewels indicating our authority. Precious stones held a special role in the adornment and enrichment of royalty. Diamonds in royal courts, the king's crowns, belts, and royal thrones are mentioned in the Bible, the Talmud and in the Midrash.

In the book, *Diamonds and Gemstones in Judaica*, it states,

> "Another article of jewellery discussed in this connection was a 'Kamra.' The Kamra was a belt made of gold and set with precious stones (Shabbat 59b) 'Such as kings do' (Rambam, Laws of the Sabbath, 19:2)".[1]

> *"And the Lord God shall save them on that day as the flock of His people, for they shall be like the stones of a crown gleaming over His land." (Zechariah 9:16).*

Stones which reflect back on their owner, as it says, as the stones of a crown glittering over His land will be seen around us.

> *"Then David took their kings crown from his head, and found it to weigh a talent of gold, and there were precious stones in it. And it was set on David's head." (1 Chronicles 20:2)*

In the prophets (Ezekiel 28:13), the wealth and pleasure of the King of Tyre are defined as follows, *"Every precious stone was thy covering."* This interpretation can be understood to mean "that all the precious stones are on his clothing."

---

1 Zvi Ilani, p.118

If we are walking in this world, in the era that God is manifesting a spiritual adorning, then as His bride, we will be adorned with jewels, as His priests, we will be adorned with jewels, and as His kings, we will be adorned with jewels.

The royal crown was not the only regal object to be ornamented with diamonds. In Jewish sources, the throne that King Solomon made in his wisdom is renowned, and we find it mentioned in the writings of 1 Kings 10:18,

> *"The king made a great throne of ivory.."* and *"was covered with precious stones and jewels". There were six steps to the throne and on each level were two lions.*[2]

> "And a mechanism would respond to the king's footsteps, and the lions would stretch out their paws to each other…And each level (step) was encrusted with precious gems, some white, some reddish, and some crystals" (Aggadic stories on the book of Esther).

It is interesting to note that many Seers today see that many of us walk with animals in the spirit realm of the Kingdom. Many see lions walking next to us, or tigers.

God will manifest jewels to adorn his kings of the earth. These stones may just appear as symbolic of adorning, or they may carry great spiritual authority.

There were even precious stones encrusted in the king's sceptre,

> *"So it was, when the king saw Queen Ester standing in the court that she found favour in his sights, and the king held out to*

---

2 Zvi Ilani, p.118

Esther the golden sceptre that was in his hand. Then Esther went near and touched the top of the sceptre." (Esther 5:2)

In the next two quotes, we see the first one revealing the craftsmanship of the angels in making our spiritual clothing as kings. And in the second one a king who is giving treasures to His son. I refer to these two quotes again, as this time, we're looking at these references in terms of kings being clothed with jewels.

In Chapter 3, we read in the quote from Pirkei Hechalot, how the angel Darniel showed him other ministering angels, who were weaving clothes of salvation, making crowns of life, brewing perfumes and sweetening wines for the righteous, who are seen as kings, like King David. [3]

Also, in Chapter 3, I shared the Midrash on the Song of Songs (Song of Song Rabba 2), about the father giving his son the precious stones and jewels, which were for Israel. And that God, the Holy One of Israel, gives His children these jewels to give us strength. [4]

This Midrash connects the representation of precious stones to strength, and that strength comes from the Torah. If we stand in God's Word, precious stones, reflect the victories we gain in His strength.

In the World to Come, we will clearly see our place and covering as kings, and here I repeat a quote I used in Chapter 3:

> "This is how the wicked shall also find the righteous on the Judgment day! The Holy One, Blessed be He says to the people of Israel, 'The wicked shall come and shall see the goodness rewarded the righteous: the people of Israel answer: They shall come and be ashamed, as it is written: 'You shall see my enemy and you shall be covered

---

3   Zvi Ilani, p.132
4   Neusner, p.85

with shame.' At this very hour, the wicked come to the entrance of the Garden of Eden, and they stand watching the goodness rewarded to the righteous, and they see all the righteous dressed in royal clothing, with royal crowns set with jewels of pearls fit for kings. And each one sits like a king on a chair of gold, and set before him is a table of pearls. And in each and everyone's hand is a golden cup inlaid with precious stones and pearls, and it is filled with the elixir of life. And all the delicacies of the Garden of Eden are placed before them, and ministering angels stand ready to serve them." (Otzar HaMirashim).[5]

Rick Joyner in his book *The Final Quest* writes,

> "As I approached the judgment seat of Christ, those in the highest ranks were also sitting on thrones that were all a part of His throne. Even the least of these thrones was more glorious than any earthly throne many times over. Some of these were rulers over the affairs of Heaven, and others over the affairs of the physical creation, such as star systems and galaxies."[6]

Jesus Himself, is the pattern for this even now, and there are a few who are fore-tasting the age to come now. Jesus is showing us how we should live and function as mature sons.

> *"So, Jesus said to them, 'Assuredly I say to you, that in the regeneration, when the Son of Man sits on the throne of His glory, you who have followed Me, will also sit on twelve thrones, judging the twelve tribes of Israel.'" (Matthew 19:28).*

---

5 Zvi Ilani, p.133
6 Justin Paul Abrahams, *Beyond Human*, Seraph Creative, 2016, p. 30

> *"Do you not know that we will judge angels?"*
> *(1 Corinthians 6:3)*

Linda Cruz in her book *All His Jewels,* says,

> "All the kings wore the best robes and beautiful crowns with jewels on them, which reflected the glory of the kingdom. The high priest wore a breast piece of judgment with twelve precious stones on it. The prophets had access to the precious stones of Urim and Thummim to help them discern the Word of the Lord. The kings wore beautiful golden crowns adorned with jewels. These three offices foreshadowed the ultimate High Priest…Jesus Christ."[7]

Jesus, as the Lord of lords and the King of kings, will adorn his mature servants who function in kingdom rule in high places. In Jesus, we are a priest, a bride, and a king, but it's one thing to inherit the offices and have them bestowed upon us; it's another thing to function and rule in them. One thing is for sure: those that do mature and function as kings, will be adorned with precious stones.

---

7   Cruz, p.126

CHAPTER NINE

Kings, Lions, Dragons, and Stones

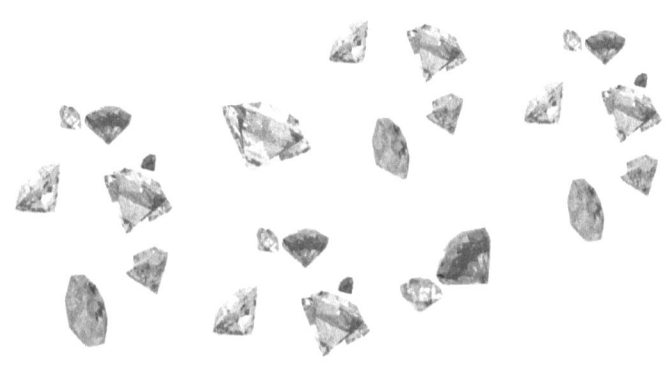

In Chapter Eight, on Believers being "kings" in the kingdom, adorned with precious stones, I mentioned that many Seers today, report that lions walk with us in the spirit. In this Chapter, I would like to expand on this concept and its relation to precious stones.

Scripture says our souls are like a well-watered garden,

> *"The Lord will guide you continually and satisfy your soul in drought, and strengthen your bones: You shall be like a watered garden, and like a spring of water, whose waters do not fail."* (Isaiah 58:11)

Our souls have their own personal ecosystem. We are constantly affecting the spiritual atmosphere around us with our thoughts, actions, and mindsets. Our renewed mind is what brings Eden around us.

Blake K. Healy, who is a recognised Seer, who sees in both worlds continually, says in his book, *The Veil: An Invitation to the Unseen Realm,*

> "In fact, we are constantly affecting the spiritual atmosphere around us with our thoughts, actions, and mindsets... Each person has an ecosystem surrounding them. These are usually a combination of giftings, thoughts, and God's presence - the spiritual surroundings that are cultivated by physical, mental life...Some of the people looked as if they are cloaked in thick blankets of warm light, crowns on their heads and swords in their hands. One guy I knew, on the far side of the room, was covered head to toe in dense green foliage, with a ring of flowing water swirling around his head."[1]

---

1   Blake K. Healy, *The Veil: An Invitation to the Unseen Realm*, Chrisma House, 2018, p. 75

We have an Eden growing around us, like a shadow or canopy flowing around us. Waterfalls and life grow around us in the spirit of the kingdom. Rivers of living healing water flow, healing jars of oil hang over us, healing tonics, healing leaves grow into us. We have lush green foliage and plants and lilies surrounding us. We shift atmospheres wherever we go, with a moving, living kingdom expanding as we steward the kingdom. We all have full access to the kingdom, but what we cultivate by our thoughts and actions, plants seeds in our garden to take dominion.

As we enlarge our hearts, the canopy of our ecosystem grows and covers more ground.

> *"I will run the course of your commandments, for you shall enlarge my heart." (Psalms 119:32)*

> *"Enlarge the place of your tent, and let them stretch out the curtains of your dwellings, do not spare, lengthen your cords, and strengthen your stakes." (Isaiah 54:2)*

If we have an Eden being built around us, which is active, would there not be rivers of precious stones flowing around us, that could manifest and adorn us? Could not angels just pick out of the rivers precious stones, and place them through the veil for us to find?

In Chapter Eight, I showed that King Solomon's throne was made of ivory and was covered with precious stones. And on the steps of this throne were two lions that watched, and in the Temple, we see these lions were engraved on the cart, we read this in 1 Kings 7:36:

> *"On the plates of its flanges and on its panels, he engraved cherubim, lions, and palm trees, wherever there was a clear space on each, with wreaths all around."*

There is a pattern: where kings function, they have lions near them and precious stones.

The Encyclopaedia Judaica says,

> "The lion is always associated with the statement of Judah, as one of the figures in the divine chariot of Ezekiel (Ezekiel 1:10)... In the Bible, there are more than 150 references to the lion, many of them descriptive, metaphoric, and allegorical. To the lion were compared the tribes of Judah (Genesis 49:9) and Dan (Deuteronomy 33:22): Balaam said of the Israelites, *"Behold a people that rise up as a lioness, and as a lion does he lift himself up"* (Numbers 23:24). The mother of the kings of Judah was compared to a lioness and her sons to lion cubs (Ezekiel 19:2-3). David, of whom it was said that his *"heart is as the heart of a lion"* (2 Samuel 17:10), declared in his lament over Saul and Jonathan, that *"they were swifter than eagles, they were stronger than lions."*[2]

The figure of the lion may have been metaphoric or allegorical, but so were just about all the elements in the temple metaphorical or allegorical. Does that mean they represent nothing real? Of course not, as the temple was a pattern of what the Heavenly kingdom and temple looked like. The creative, living realms of Heaven are real.

I know of three people who have spiritual animals that walk with them. I have a lion that walks with me, and of the other two, one has a tiger, and the other has a dragon. You may look at the last one and think, "a 'dragon' are you mad?" Nope! There are spiritual animals of the kingdom that walk in our cultivated Edens, that act as guardians. For in Eden, there were guardian creatures that watched. We have angels and guardian creatures that follow us.

---

2 www.bjeindy.org - The Encyclopaedia Judaica

In the Jubilee Bible translation, it uses the word tiger instead of leopard, which many Bible translation use. But either way, it shows there are spiritual animals that God likens his actions too. God is even compared to a bear, and sometimes, God's spiritual agents manifest His actions.

> *"Therefore, I will be unto them as a lion, as a tiger in the way I will observe them."* (Hosea 13:7)

> *"Therefore, a lion from the forest shall slay them, a wolf of the desert shall destroy them, a tiger will watch over the cities…"* (Jeremiah 5:6)

I will admit in these verses the animals are described as going out to war to destroy wickedness, but this in no way disproves that they cannot be guardians that protect us under God's orders.

What about the dragons in the Bible? If one studies the ancient interpretations of the Seraphim Angels, they will find that they were described as flying serpent-like dragons.

> *"Above it, stood Seraphim, each one had six wings, with two, he covered his face, with two, he covered his feet, and with two he flew."* (Isaiah 6:2)

In later chapters of the book of Isaiah, when *"Sarap"* appears alongside the Hebrew verb *"Uph"* for "flying", it is rendered *"fiery, flying serpent"* – dragon (Isaiah 14:29 and 30:6).

We are a walking Eden on the earth, and our atmosphere in the kingdom is ever growing around us. If God's kingdom interacts with us, there is no reason why precious stones cannot manifest to adorn us, or that spiritual guardians cannot live in our little Edens.

CHAPTER TEN

Symbolic Memorial Stones!

In the book of Joshua, it gives symbolic hints, of eternal rewards being dropped as memorial stones, which they carry into the promised land. Shari Abbott in her article, *A Stone of Deliverance and Memorial in Joshua*, says:

> "Joshua chapter three, tells us of God miraculously leading His people through the Jordan River into the Promised Land. Just as God had parted the Red Sea and delivered His people out of bondage in Egypt, He also parted the waters of the Jordan and delivered His people from the wilderness journey, into the land that He had promised.
>
> "God gave clear instructions about how the river crossing would take place. With the waters parted, the priests were instructed to walk halfway across, carrying the Ark of the Covenant. They were to stop in the midst of the riverbed and allow the people to cross over to the other side on dry ground.
>
> "Typologically, this was an example of the Ark (representing God) going before them and holding back the waters (a symbol of God's mercy). This leading into the Promised Land, is symbolic of our safe passage into Heaven because we belong to Jesus, who is our Ark and He withheld the flood of God's judgement from us, by taking it upon Himself on the cross. God commanded that their crossing over the river Jordan was to be memorialized with a memorial on the shore of the Jordan. Once again, it was to be a memorial built with stones.
>
> "God instructed Joshua that, when the people reached the other side of the Jordan, he was to appoint a man from every tribe (twelve men, Joshua 4:2). Each man would select a stone from the dry ground in the midst of the riverbed, where the priests' feet stood firm (Joshua 4:3). They were to carry the stones to the shore and "leave them in the lodging place" (Joshua 4:3) where

they would spend the night. Each of the twelve men carried a stone upon his shoulder and did as Joshua instructed. Joshua explained to the people the reason for this.

> *"That this may be a sign among you when your children you in time to come, saying, 'What do these stones mean to you?' Then you shall answer them that the waters of Jordan were cut off before the Ark of the Covenant of the Lord: when it crossed over Jordan, the waters of Jordan were cut off: and these stones shall be for a memorial unto the children of Israel forever." (Joshua 4:6-7)*

"This memorial of twelve stones served as a witness to God's deliverance of His people."[1]

They carried victory stones, deliverance stones, as they were lead in God's presence (behind the Ark of His presence) to the other side, to set up memorial stones. They carried their stones into the promised land: they carried them into Heaven symbolically. Their walking through the river symbolized the walking out of their lives on earth. These stones will stand forever as memorial stones in Heaven.

> *"The wall of the City had twelve foundation stones, and on them were written the names of the twelve apostles of the Lamb" (Revelation 21:14)*

> *"I will lay your battlements (victories) of rubies, your gates of sparkling jewels, and all your walls of precious stones." (Isaiah 54:12)*

---

[1] Shari Abbot, *Reasons for Hope: A Stone of Deliverance and memorial in Joshua* - https://reasonsforhopejesus.com/7-stone-deliverance-memorial-joshua/

All victories will shine in Heaven as we are all living stones with testimonies rewarded/recorded in the walls of Salvation.

Many of the stones manifesting today are symbolic victory stones, stones of deliverance and accomplishments. These stones we are to carry with us as memorial stones.

CHAPTER ELEVEN

Stones of Function: Lion, Man, Ox, Eagle

The Stones on the Priest's breastplate did not just represent the twelve tribes of Israel, but also their function in God. Within the border were twelve stones set in gold, arranged in rows of four, and like those in the shoulder pieces, were engraved with the names of the tribe. Each precious stone served as a brand or signature of a person or tribe.

Thus, we read,

> *"The children of Israel shall pitch by his own standard with the ensign of their father's house." (Numbers 2:2,34)*

The term "ensign" indicates a token of the Divine Will or Presence.

The twelve tribes, excluding the Levites, were grouped into four camps. Each of these groups of the tribes was to rally around the tribal standard of the leading tribe, according to their function. Each tribe was represented on the breastplate, and each stone spoke of their function in the kingdom.

Judah's tribal standard was the Lion, Reuben's ensign was a Man, Ephraim's the Ox, and Dan's the Eagle. These stood as functions and spiritual (service) callings.

It's interesting to note that these four primary tribal standards, the Lion, the Man, the Ox, and the Eagle, are the same as the four faces of the strange living creatures (super angels, called Cherubim) that appear surrounding the throne of God.[1]

The four emblems symbolic of Christ's life ministry were placed by God within and around the Tabernacle. So, we have Christ's nature, represented by the four living creatures (angels) in Heaven, then corresponding to the four main camps around the Tabernacle

---

[1] Chuck Missler, Hidden *Treasures in the Biblical Text*. Koinonia House 2000, p.66-68

on earth, grouping the rest of the twelve tribes, which were in one of the four camps ensigned with a divine function. These divine functions are also represented in the twelve stones on the breastplate of the priest.

The four camps and their stones represented their functions, and the other tribes who sat in one of the four camps, their stones spoke of their characters.

The stones on the priest's breastplate represented the twelve tribes of Israel and all the children of God that would ever exist. All the children of God are grouped with a spiritual function of the Divine Will and Presence.

This gives us the connection between – "Precious Stones" speaking about our functions, victories, character traits, strengths, and weaknesses, in relation to the gemstones that are manifesting today. It also shows that some precious stones' functions are connected to angels. The living creatures and their angelic ranks support the functions of the tribe's callings.

Leslie Hardinge in his book *Stones of Fire* says of the twelve stones,

> "These pairs of twelve characters embrace every possible nature found among men, both in weakness and strength. Perfected, these prototypes reach the ultimate goal God purposed for mankind. Through the Twelve Gates, all the redeemed will have to pass. Upon the Twelve Foundations alone will they be able to stand unmoved… The purpose of God in inscribing each of the tribes and apostles on an appropriate precious stone, was that the quality of the gems should act as a foil, to show off the peculiar lustre of their individual natures.

These Foundations were designed to help every man to let his light so shine."[2]

The people of God that make up the Twelve Tribes and the Twelve Apostles may be represented by the four emblems of the Lion, the Man, the Ox, and the Eagle.

Leslie Hardinge says,

> "The Lion is the king of beasts. It is a fearless leader of the animals. The Man is typical of that which is outstanding in him when compared with other living creatures or things upon this earth. He has sympathy and understanding love. The Ox speaks to us of patient, toiling sacrifice, while the Eagle tells us of soaring vision."

These emblems speak of even more; it speaks of those who are spiritual Kings in the Kingdom who do spiritual warfare, Priests who are intercessors, Seers, Prophets, Servants, Leaders, Saints who carry sympathy, sacrifice, revelation, and kingdom functions.

> *"The four living creatures sang a new song saying, 'Thou art worthy to take the book and open the seals thereof, for thou was slain, and has redeemed us to God by the blood out of every kindred, and tongue, and people, and nation. And has made us unto our God kings and priests, and we shall reign on the earth'."*
> *(Revelation 5:8-10)*

We are being transformed and made partakers of the Divine Nature (2 Peter 1:4). As we yield to God's Spirit, we are conformed to His image, but also our functions and callings bring out a measure of Heaven's governmental rule and reign into the earth.

---

2 Haringe, p. 38

The priest was adorned with stones that spoke, and as priests, our stones speak about us!

The priest's garments represented the cosmos and the Heavenly realm. The breastplate stones represented the twelve tribes of Israel, the children of God, the twelve constellations, and the twelve Heavenly governmental houses.

> *"Then God said, let there be light in the firmament of the Heavens to divide the day from the night, and let them be for signs, and seasons, and for days and years." (Genesis 1:14)*

The stones spoke of the children of God, connected with the twelve constellations to be signs speaking about their seasons, days and years. The stones also spoke of their functions and characters traits. The stones were revelation stones of the children of God. They even spoke of their births, as in Birthstones.

> *"Then you shall take two onyx stones and engrave on them the names of the sons of Israel, six of their names on one stone and six on the other stone, in order of their birth." (Exodus 28:9-10)*

> "In the four rows of the stones was the glory of the father's. The glory of the fathers is the blessing upon Abraham's seeds that would result in blessing to the whole world." (G.K. Beale)

The stones represented all those who would be children of God. Not only that, they spoke of all the children of God that were in Heavenly realms, yet to be born, and their seasons, functions, days and years on earth.

As I have mentioned, as Believers in Christ, as a priest, as a bride, and as a king, we are being adorned with our stones (or many are experiencing this foretaste). The stones manifesting today, speak of us, some as a priest, some as love stones adorning us as a bride, and some as a king, in kingly positions of authority. As all of us have been called with giftings and functions to establish governmental rule into the earth, our stones will reflect this and grow as we mature. And as the four living creatures overflow the Divine Presence (from out of God) into the twelve Heavenly governmental houses to be administrated to the individual earthly camps (our ministries), some stones will be graced and be empowering stones. Grace and empowering stones in the sense that they come with an angel to achieve God's work in us. For God's presence carries GRACE!

As Living Stones in eternity, living in the heart of God before the creation of the world, we were sent and appointed to earth with a calling and function. Our days and years were written and ordained for us. And as Believers, our Heavenly stones in the Heavens that are formed, and those revealed, as in manifesting in the earth, represent us in physical precious stones. Stones that change and transform as God's will and nature are established in us.

For all our works, functions, services will be judged as of *"Gold, Silver and Precious Stones"* (1 Corinthians 3:12-15).

The following verses show our journey from stepping out of God as living spirits (living stones), with our decreed destinies into the earth. And as our lives unfold in the earth, spiritual stones form and represent us. They hold and carry our transformations as we reflect the Kingdom, changing with our seasons, functions, and giftings.

> *"Before I formed you in the womb, I knew you; before you were born, I set you apart: I appointed you as a prophet to the nations." (Jeremiah 1:5)*

> *"Your eyes saw my unformed body; all the days ordained for me were written in your book before one of them came to be." (Psalm 139:16)*
>
> *From one man he made all the nations, that they should inhabit the whole earth; and he marked out their appointed times in history and the boundaries of their lands." (Acts 17:26)*

You came from Heaven through one of the twelve gates,

"It had a great high wall with twelve gates and with twelve angels at the gates." (Revelation 21:12) – Predestined, *"He predestined us for adoption to sonship through Jesus Christ."* (Ephesians 1:5)

The twelve Zodiac signs are the twelve gates (Revelation 21:12), but are also connected to the twelve governmental councillor houses in Heaven. This copy is played out on earth –

> *"The Children of Israel shall pitch by his own standard with the ensign of their father's houses." (Numbers 2:34)*
>
> *"And the intricately woven band of the Ephod, which is on it, shall be of the same workmanship, made of gold, blue, purple, and scarlet thread, and fine woven linen. Then you shall take two onyx stones and engrave on them the names of the sons of Israel, six of their names on one stone and six names on the other stone, in order of their birth." (Exodus 28:8-10)*

This reminds me of "birth stones". Now, I'm certainly not pushing New Age, but if the stones on the breastplate speak of the children of God, and also the zodiac, (stars/lights in the sky), as Scripture says in Genesis, are for seasons, years and days, I believe these stones are talking about the days and seasons of the children of Israel, and then they could include their birth in the stones' reflection.

"And God said, 'Let there be lights in the firmament of the Heavens to divide the day from the night, and let them be for signs, and for seasons, and for days, and years.'" (Genesis 1:14)

The word "Zodiac" means 'circle of living creatures.'[3] The four "Living Creatures" around the throne look like a Lion, a Man, an Ox, and an Eagle. These creatures are angels that reflect the nature of God.

The four main tribes of Israel – Judah, Reuben, Ephraim, & Dan – were given the emblems around the earthly Tabernacle of the Lion, the Man, the Ox, and the Eagle.

Each one of these tribes/emblems was represented with a precious stone on the Priest's breastplate. The other tribes fitted into one of those four camps – sitting under the function of the emblem.

The four precious stones represented functions, the Lion, the Man, the Ox, and the Eagle, and the other eight precious stones represented character traits and strengths. All of the stones spoke in some way of God's nature.

The stones representing the twelve signs of the Zodiac all spoke of the Children of God, their journeys through the seasons of life. The stones were revelation stones of the Children of God.

---

3   http://www.thefullwiki.org/Zodiac - The word zodiac comes from the Latin word "zōdiacus", which comes from the Greek word "ζῳδιακὸς κύκλος", which means circle of animals. Retrieved June 2019

CHAPTER TWELVE

The Full Face of God in Stone

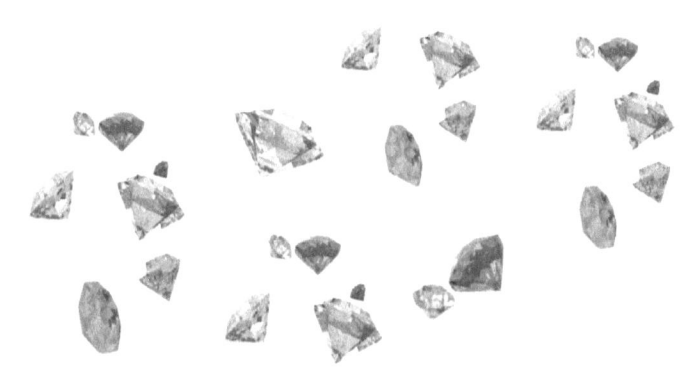

In this Chapter, the main insights and points of the last Chapter are gathered together and listed. This helps to clearly focus in on the connections. The connections between tribes, priests, children of God, and angels with their relationship with the stones. The stones have multiple interpretations of revelation.

- ❖ God pours His divine presence and nature upon the four living creatures around the throne.
- ❖ These four living creatures have the faces of a Lion, a Man, an Ox, and an Eagle.
- ❖ These living creatures are like "Super Angels", called Cherubim, which protect God's throne and holiness.
- ❖ We also encounter the four faces in the key roles among the tribal standards/functions of the twelve tribes of Israel.
- ❖ The angels who are ministering spirits of God, function in helping God's nature be established in His people.
- ❖ There were four camps around the earthly Tabernacle emblems representing, a Lion, a Man, an Ox, and an Eagle. Each of these groups comprised of three tribes each (4 x 3 = 12).
- ❖ The Priest's breastplate had twelve stones on it, representing the twelve tribes of Israel,, the children of God and all those who were not yet born.
- ❖ Four of those stones represented kingdom functions, while the other eight represented kingdom characters and gifts to match. All the stones speak of God's nature.
- ❖ The four tribes of the emblems, Judah – Lion, Reuben – Man, Ephraim – Ox, Dan – Eagle, had Super-Angels assigned to their functions (the four living creatures).
- ❖ The twelve tribes all had angels assigned to their callings (Revelation 21:12).
- ❖ The stones on the priest's breastplate also represented the twelve constellation signs. The word "Zodiac" in Greek means "living creature" – which relates to angels.

- ❖ The twelve stones, representing the twelve tribes and children of God, all had angels assigned to them. *"It had a great, high wall with twelve gates, and with twelve angels at the gates. On the gates were written the names of the twelve tribes of Israel."* (Revelation 21:12)
- ❖ The Israelites were to camp under their respective banners beside the flags of their families. (Numbers 2:2)
- ❖ The Priest's garments represented the cosmos and the Heavenly realms.
- ❖ The precious stones on the breastplate, spoke of functions, and also the constellation signs, which spoke of the children's seasons, days and years (Genesis 1:14).
- ❖ Today – in this season of God manifesting stones, angels are bringing precious stones to adorn Kingdom functions: Priest, Bride, Lord & King – (four functions – working out the four faces of the full nature of God).

The stones – speak of us, as children of God. They are revelation stones of who we are and what we carry. As Living Stones (Believers) – (1 Peter 2:5) – We also have angels assigned to us. (Matthew 18:10)

CHAPTER THIRTEEN

The Eternal Breastplate -
The City on the Heart of God

In this Chapter, we will look at the relationship between God's city and his heart-beat, and also our representation in the New Jerusalem city.

The eternal city is the same shape as the priest's breastplate on earth (square/cube). God holds His city, His children on His heart. This shape is also the form of the holies of holies, a cube, so we, in fact, live in the heart of the Most Holy God.

God's life and light shine through the children of God, as they are "Living Stones" fitted into the heart of God. For there is no other foundation that can be laid (1 Corinthians 3:11).

> *"Having been built on the foundation of the apostles and prophets, Jesus Christ Himself being the chief cornerstone, in whom the whole building, being joined together, grows into a holy temple in the Lord." (Ephesians 2:20-22)*

As "Living Stones" we are being fitted and locked into the city, with our room (mansion).

We came out of God to be established in God. As the children of God mature and come to perfection, we will reflect the four functions of God and His full face (nature), shining the qualities of the emblems of the Lion, the Man, the Ox, and the Eagle.

These functions and qualities and natures, won't just be perfected in us, they will be represented in memorial stones in the walls of the city. These memorial stones are tested stones that hold and speak of the DNA of our works, established in Him by grace.

As we stand before the throne and our works get tested by fire, what remains, gold, silver and precious stones (1 Corinthians 3), will be revealed to us as we walk into the Kingdom, through the twelve gates into the eternal city. We will see our memorial stones fitted in the walls of the city in gold sockets, with silver cement, silver glory!

The walls are made of pure gold, with gold sockets studded in them. These sockets hold our memorial stones that will shine in the city as a testimony to our works done in him. As the precious stones speak of us, the gold sockets speak of us as being united, encased in the divine nature, and the silver speaks of us being cemented and made as one union in Him. Silver was used as cement in building the temple. And silver also speaks of us, as the "spirit man" who accomplishes the works. For Scripture says our spirit is like a silver cord, *"Before the silver cord is snapped…and the spirit returns to God who gave it."* (Ecclesiastes 12:6-7) And then locked in the silver cement is the expression of the quality of our works represented in precious stones. *"If anyone builds on this foundation using gold, silver, precious stones, his work will be shown for what it is"* (1 Corinthians 3:12). This shows us these stones represent us united in Him, in the gold sockets in God's city.

As we are adorned in fullness as a priest, a bride, a lord and a king, we will walk into the city with honour as we see the different glories the children of God have attained (1 Corinthians 15:41).

Jonathan Edwards, in his book *Charity and Its Fruits,* describes how we will reflect on seeing our different glories in the saints:

> "And besides the inferior in glory will have no temptation to envy those that are higher than themselves, for those that are highest will not only be more loved by the lower for their higher holiness, but they will also have more of the spirit of love to others, and so will love those that are below them more than if their own capacity and elevation were less. They that are highest in degree in glory will be of the highest capacity; and so having the greatest knowledge, will see most of God's loveliness, and consequently will have love to God and love to the saints most abounding in their hearts. And on this account, those that are lower in glory will not envy those that are above them, because they will be most loved by those that are highest in glory. And the

superior in glory will be so far from slighting those that are inferior, that they will have the most abundant love toward them – greater degrees of love in proportion to their superior knowledge and happiness. The higher any are in glory, the more they are like Christ in this respect, so that the love of the equals of the latter to them."[1]

As we walk into the city as perfected "Living Stones", standing on the foundation of God's heart, in the city of gold, we will see the manifold wisdom of God's Grace studded in the walls of His city, revealing Him in us. The stones have always spoken of us, the children of God. The word "manifold" means "many coloured"[2] and highlights the many coloured stones and their achievements. The colours of the rainbow of glory will radiate throughout Heaven.

> *"By wisdom, a house is built, and through understanding, it is established, through knowledge its rooms are filled with rare and beautiful treasures" (Proverbs 24:3-4)*

> *"Now it shall come to pass in the latter days, that the Mountain of the Lord's House shall be established on top of the Mountains, And shall be exalted above the hills; And peoples shall flow to it. Many nations shall come and say, "Come, and let us go up to the Mountain of the Lord." (Micah 4:1-2)*

All that does not represent the city and the heartbeat of God will be left out.

---

[1] Jonathan Edwards, *Charity and Its Fruits*, The Banner Of Truth, 2005, p. 337.
[2] https://biblehub.com/commentaries/edt/1_peter/4.htm referring to 1 Peter 4:10, the word "manifold" actually means "variegated", and this source gives a deeper understanding of the word. Retrieved June 2019

"Outside the city, are the dogs, the sorcerers, the sexually immoral, the murderers, the idol worshipers, and all who love to live a lie." (Revelation 22:15)

Jesus said in My Father's house are many mansions (rooms) – (John 14). As Believers, we are "Living Stones" of the Heavenly Temple (1 Peter 2:5). We each occupy a room (some mansions/palaces). In our room is placed our treasures, rewards, and gifts. Our pure works (1 Corinthians 3:11-15) and victories will be studded in the "walls of Salvation" (Isaiah 45:12) That is why we must be careful how we build (1 Corinthians 3:10).

"For we are God's handiwork, created in Christ Jesus to do good works, which God prepared in advance for us to do." (Ephesians 2:10)

"Great is the Lord, and greatly to be praised in the city of our God, the mountains of His holiness. Beautiful in elevation, the joy of the whole earth is Mount Zion on the sides of the north, the city of the great King. God is known in her palaces for a refuge" (Psalms 48:1-3)

"Walk about Zion, and go all around her. Count her towers; Mark well her bulwarks, consider her Palaces, that you may tell it to the generation following. For this is God, Our God forever and ever, He will be our guide even to death." (Psalms 48:12-14)

"In that day this song will be sung in the land of Judah; We have a strong city; God makes salvation its walls and ramparts." (Isaiah 26:1)

"No longer will violence be heard in your land, nor ruin or destruction within your borders, but you will call your Walls Salvation and your gates Praise." (Isaiah 60:18)

> *"O you afflicted one, tossed with tempest and not comforted, behold I will lay your stones with colourful gems, And lay your foundations with sapphires. I will make your pinnacles of rubies, Your gates of crystal, And all your walls of precious stones." (Isaiah 54:11-12)*

> *"He who overcomes I will make a pillar in the temple of my God, and he shall go no more out; and I will write upon him the name of my God, and the name of the city of my God, which is New Jerusalem, which comes down out of Heaven from my God; and I will write upon him my new name." (Revelation 3:12)*

> *"I saw the Holy City, the New Jerusalem, coming down out of Heaven from God, prepared as a bride beautifully dressed for her husband." (Revelation 21:2)*

Your literal heartbeat, imprints of love, your works done unto the King – sacrifices and victories are being written/studded into the walls of the Heavenly city. Our presence of love is structured as a remembrance in the walls of the city with precious stones, which we are merited by working in His Grace. The city can be called the "Bride" adorned (with jewels) because the walls shine and reflect the presence of the body of Christ (from all ages); their love for Him. The city's DNA – is the treasure of the frequency of all Believers. The city is a Bride of which the "Living Stones" (us) – will dwell inside her heart-beat, in our rooms (mansions). God created the walls (heart, foundation), and placed "us" to beat life in it with our presence.

> *"And I saw the holy city, New Jerusalem, coming down out of Heaven from God, prepared as a Bride adorned for her husband." (Revelation 21:2)*

As in the Old Testament, the people of God brought precious stones to build the temple, now in the New, the people of God in

Christ are meriting their stones, and bringing them into the temple in Heaven. We see this in the Old Testament in 1 Chronicles:

> *"And whoever had precious stones gave them to the treasury of the house of the Lord, in the care of Jehiel the Gershonite. Then the people rejoiced because they had given willingly, for with a whole heart they had offered freely to the Lord." (1 Chronicles 29:8-9)*

> *"Lord our God, all this abundance that we have provided for building you a temple for your holy name comes from your hand, and all of it belongs to you. I know, my God, that you test the heart and are pleased with integrity. All these things I have given willingly and with honest intent. And now I have seen with joy how willingly your people who are here have given to you. Lord, the God of our fathers Abraham, Isaac, and Israel, keep these desires and thoughts in the hearts of your people forever and keep their hearts loyal to you. And give my son Solomon the wholehearted devotion to keep your commands, statutes, and decrees and to do everything to build the palatial structure for which I have provided." (1 Chronicles 29:16-19)*

Verse 16 says: *"That we have prepared to build you a house, and you test the hearts and have pleasure in uprightness."* This is now in reverse – We are not building an earthly temple, but a spiritual one (1 Peter 2:5 – Living Stones). As our hearts are tested with the willingness to "freely" love with "integrity", "honesty", and "devotion"; the treasure of our hearts (Matthews 6:21), which God works in us, is building and preparing the walls of Salvation (Isaiah 55:12) of the Heavenly temple.

> *"For no one can lay a foundation other than the one already laid, which is Jesus Christ. If anyone builds on this foundation using gold, silver, precious stones, wood, hay, or straw, his workmanship will be evident, because the day will bring it to*

light. It will be revealed with fire, and the fire will prove the quality of each man's work." (1 Corinthians 3:12)

Your pure works in Him, are building the spiritual temple, you are building, as a living stone in the temple, your room (Palace), which is one part of the whole temple which your Father is preparing for you.

"I will greatly rejoice in the Lord, my soul shall be joyful in my God; for He has clothed me with the garments of Salvation, He has covered me with a robe of righteousness, as a bridegroom decks Himself with ornaments, and as a bride adorns herself with her jewels." (Psalms 19:5)

CHAPTER FOURTEEN

Stones of Fire: Hidden in the Heartbeat of God

What were the Stones of Fire in Ezekiel 28:12-16? And what was this dwelling place that Lucifer on the Mountain of God walked among these fiery stones? To answer these questions, we must go beyond God's throne and into His heartbeat.

The most powerful angels were allowed to come up to the throne and entered through (the throne), walking on a pavement of fire. There these angels could walk and go deep inside God to His very heartbeat. This was God's house, the holiest and most powerful place in existence. It was the highway into the heart of God, the path of righteousness and immortality.

"In the way of righteousness there is life: along that path is immortality" (Proverbs 12:28) – "And a highway will be there, it will be called the Way of holiness; it will be for those who walk on that Way. The unclean will not journey on it; wicked fools will not go about on it." (Isaiah 35:8) On either side of this highway path were precious stones, stones of glistening fire. These stones adorned and covered Lucifer. They covered him in two ways, the first being the rays of light from the stones on either side of the highway path around God's heart shone into him as he walked to communicate with God. And the second way Lucifer covered was that stones were placed into him. Lucifer and many angels would go deep into the heartbeat of God to receive and then minister the mysteries of God. Inside were thrones, seats of gods, where divine councils took place.

Lucifer's role, who is said to have "covered" the stones of fire, was to go right up and engage these stones, where the very pulsating presence of God would vibrate through flames of fire over and around the stones. The stones held the mysteries of God, there were stones of Love, Wisdom, Knowledge, Power, Might, Holiness, and Beauty, and so on, revealing the whole council of God's nature.

As Lucifer, pure and transparent, yielded into the presence that vibrated and pulsated from the stones, he received the mysteries and knowledge and character traits of God's nature. He was the seal of perfection because the mind and heart of God consumed him and filled his being while he covered the stones. In his reflecting of the nature of God, precious stones were placed into his mountings on his breastplate. Lucifer's breastplate was a symbol of the seal of his perfection. The breastplate represented with its covering of stones, what he had been adorned with, and what he carried in his mind and heart. In other words, what had been infused into him from God. He had been transformed by the renewing of his mind and heart.

The name Lucifer means the *bringer of light*, or the *light bearer*. It was Lucifer's role to absorb the DNA of God from the stones and reflect them into the universe. It was to be his role as a ministering spirit guardian to reveal revelation to the other angels, and to drop revelation into the universe for mankind to catch in their spirits. There were twelve stones of fire, but Lucifer's seal of perfection was sealed with the infusion of nine. Twelve were to be infused into mankind, fully transforming them into the image and likeness of God. The number twelve is the number that represents full government and reign. Twelve stones of fire, twelve stones on Adam's breastplate, twelve stones on the priest's breastplate, twelve tribes, twelve apostles, and twelve foundations stones in the Heavenly Jerusalem. By entering the fire transformation and likeness was obtained. This was like a baptism of fire. Today is no different, we catch mysteries from God by the infusion of revelation.

The twelve stones of fire hold layers of revelation and open up dimensions of learning. These stones are also connected to the twelve governmental councillor houses in Heaven that administer tokens of the Divine Will. These include resources and functions to do with divine laws of ruling in the kingdom. The copy on earth of these houses is seen in Numbers 2:34.

As the Son (Jesus) shone the Father's glory (Hebrews 1:3), and God clothes Himself in garments of light (Psalms 104), so too, Adam and Eve's righteousness was the radiating glory that robed them, as they were created in the image of God. The glory that clothed their spirits, shone through their dust-formed bodies, like robes of light. They were naked, but not ashamed, as the glory clothed them. When Adam and Eve sinned, those glory-garments lifted, faded, and there they stood, naked, in flesh-and-blood bodies, and they ran for cover. This is why I believe Adam functioned as the first King and Priest adorned with jewels - being in the image of God - the King of kings and Lord (Priest) of lords. There are Rabbinical writings that support this.[1]

These stones, living stones inside God, (all that God is), was the light and illumination that shone out of God, shining like a rainbow over the throne of glory. God's perfect light was shining out of Him like flames of fire, reflecting in the precious stones, manifesting all the colours of glory.

> *"There was a rainbow around the throne, in the appearance like an emerald." (Revelation 4:3)*

In the book of Ezekiel 28:12-16, it speaks about Lucifer walking in the midst of the stones of fire:

> *"You were the seal of perfection, full of wisdom and perfect in beauty. You were in Eden, the garden of God; every precious stone adorned you, carnelian, chrysolite, and emerald, topaz, onyx and jasper, lapis lazuli, turquoise and beryl. Your settings and*

---

[1] Targum Pseudo-Yonathan on Genesis 27:15; B. Pesahim 54a; Genesis Rabbah 20:12; Numbers Rabbah 4:8; Pesikta de-Rabbi Eliezer 20:46a, 22:50b; Pesikta de-Rav Kahana; Pesikta Rabbati 37; Midrash Tanhuma, Toledot 12; Aggadat Bereshit, Sefer ha-Zikhronot 1:3; Zohar 1:53a, 1:73b-74a, 2:229b; Ben Yehoyada; Shi nei Luhot ha-B'rit, va - yeshev; Kedushat Shabbat 5:13b." (*Tree of Souls* p. 438)

> *mountings were made of gold, on the day you were created they were prepared. You were anointed as a guardian cherub, for so I ordained you. You were on the holy mount of God; you walked among the fiery stones. You were blameless in your way from the day you were created till wickedness was found in you. Through your widespread trade, you were filled with violence, and you sinned. So, I drove you in disgrace from the mount of God, and I expelled you, guardian cherub from among the fiery stones."*

Ezekiel 28:2 speaks of the "seat of the gods", this is the place of the divine council where the most powerful angels and creatures came and communicate with God,

> *"This is what the Sovereign LORD says, 'In the pride of your heart you say, I am a god, I sit on the throne of a god in the heart of the seas'."*

Lucifer did sit on a throne like a god, for there are thrones in the council, but it was his attitude that swelled with pride that was his downfall. When it says, "heart of the seas", it is speaking about a very lofty place above the firmament of the universe.

Micheal Heiser writes in his book *The Unseen Realm*,

> "Both phrases, 'seat of the gods' and 'heart of the seas', point to the place of divine authority, the throne room of the divine council."[2]

Psalm 89:5-7 also speaks and gives light on this divine council in the heart of God,

> *"Let the Heavens praise your wonders, O Lord, your faithfulness in the assembly of the holy ones! For who in the skies can be*

---

2 Michael S. Heiser *The Unseen Realm: Recovering the supernatural worldview of the Bible*, Leham Press, 2015, p. 76

compared to the Lord? Who among the Heavenly beings is like the Lord, a God greatly to be feared in the council of the holy ones and awesome above all who are around him."

Isaiah 14:12 shows us that Lucifer had his own throne,

"How you have fallen from Heaven, O Morning Star, son of the dawn! You have been cut down to the ground, O destroyer of nations. You said in your heart, I will ascend to the Heavens; I will raise my throne above the stars of God. I will sit on the mount of assembly, in the far reaches of the north..."

These passages reveal to us that Lucifer walked in the midst of the fiery stones. Also, that he sat on a throne in the assembly of the divine councils. And that he sat right up close to God's throne and walked down the pavement of the stones of fire to receive mysteries and impartations from the vibrating precious stones in God's heartbeat. This is where he covered the stones of fire, and he was adorned with the light of God. As he became those qualities, he gained the seal of perfection infused, and was adorned with nine stones.

In the Book of Enoch, it describes God's house of fire, the inner heart of God,

"And I beheld a vision...there was a second house, greater than the former...and it was built of flames of fire, and its floor was of fire, and above it were lightnings and the path of the stars, and its ceiling also was flaming fire. And I looked and saw therein a lofty throne; its appearance was as crystal and the wheels thereof as the shining sun, and there was the vision of cherubim. And from underneath the throne came streams of flaming fire so that I could not look thereon. And the Great Glory sat thereon, and His raiment shone more brightly than the sun...the flaming fire

was around about Him, and a great fire stood before Him." (1 Enoch 14:15-22)[3]

The Book of Enoch goes on to reveal about the precious stones of fire, which in them held the secrets of God. Enoch talks of being shown in a vision the secrets of righteousness and mercy; these were part of the precious stones in God's heart. They contained the mysteries of God:

> *"Afterwards, my spirit was concealed, ascending into the Heavens. I beheld the sons of the holy angels treading on flaming fire, whose garments and robes were white, and whose countenances were transparent as crystal. I saw two rivers of fire glittering like the hyacinth. Then I fell on my face before the Lord of Spirits.* **And Michael, one of the archangels, took me by the right hand, raised me up, and brought me out to where was every secret of mercy and secret of righteousness. He showed me all the hidden things of the extremities of Heaven**, *all the receptacles of the stars, and the splendours of all, from whence they went forth, before the face of the holy. And he concealed the spirit of Enoch in the Heaven of Heavens. There I beheld, in the midst of that light, a building raised with stones of ice. And in the midst of the stones, vibrations of living fire. My spirit saw around the circle of this flaming habitation, on one of its extremities, that there was a river full of living fire which encompassed it." (Enoch 70: 1-8)*[4] (emphasis mine)

Where Enoch talks of stones of ice, this is a reference to looking like crystal, like burning white light, and in the midst of this habitation were stones absorbing the frequency of the vibrating

---

3 David Humphries, *The Lost Book of Enoch*, Cambridge Media Group, 2006.
4 Humphries

flames of fire imprinting the secrets of God into the precious stones of fire. Precious stones hold frequencies, energies, and vibrations of coded mysteries.

We have seen throughout this book, that wherever stones show up, they are representing us nearby. It is here in the heart of God, where we came from and first lived. For Enoch goes on to say,

> *"Then that angel came to me, and with his voice saluted me, saying 'they are the offspring of a man, who are born for righteousness'." (1 Enoch 14:17)*[5]

We are created in God's image, perfect before we come to earth. As living stones, the stones of fire reflect God's nature, and they reflect us. Lucifer covered the stones of fire to be like God in character, but he also covered us as living spirits in God's heart, for he was our guardian over us.

There is a general agreement in rabbinic lore that the souls of the unborn are kept in a storehouse or Treasury of Souls. The Treasury is found under the Throne of Glory, and a dazzling brilliant light emanates from the many souls in repose there. Those souls are in their pristine state, untainted by existence in this world. Some of them flicker like a small candle and some shine like a torch.[6]

When the Lord created Adam and Eve, before He formed them on earth, God created them in His person to spend their first stay of life with Him, not on the planet but in Heaven. They had not yet received their clay bodies; it came after their first communion with

---

5 Humphries
6 Howard Schwartz, *Tree of Souls: The Mythology of Judaism*, Oxford University Press, P.166

their Maker. The Book of Genesis says the Lord made them on day six and formed them on day eight.[7]

Lucifer teaches us many lessons for us to watch out for, that we do not close our hearts off to God's revelations. He also shows many parallels with our walk. We must yield into God's heart and know that the stones speak about God's nature becoming ours, as sons and daughters of God.

- ❖ He was after God's own heart" (Acts 13:22). As Lucifer was close to God's heart at the beginning, so can we learn, we are to be close to God's heart as David was.
- ❖ We are to have one heart and have a new spirit infused into us." (Ezekiel 11:19-21) As Lucifer covered the stones of fire, God's presence infused into him. This is a lesson we can learn: we are to come unto God, be born again and have our spirit infused with the presence of God, as we engage Him.
- ❖ *"For where our treasure is, our heart will be also."* (Matthews 6:21) – As Lucifer covered the stones of fire and us (we are Gods treasure), we can learn from Lucifer that where we place our heart, our treasure will be found in God's heart, yielding to His nature.
- ❖ *"My son, if you receive my words, and treasure my commands within you, So that you incline your ear to wisdom, and apply your heart to understanding; Yes, if you cry out for discernment, and lift up your voice for understanding, if you seek her as silver, and search for her as for hidden treasures; Then you will understand the fear of the Lord, and find the knowledge of God."* (Proverbs 2:1-5)
- ❖ Lucifer found wisdom covering the stones of fire; if we seek God and his presence, we too, will find wisdom.
- ❖ *"And to make plain to everyone the administration of this mystery, which for ages was kept hidden in God, who created all things. His intent was that now, through the Church, the manifold wisdom of God*

---

[7] Paula A. Price, PhD. *Before the Garden: God's Eternal Continuum*. Flaming Vision Publications, 2014, p.75

should be made known to the rulers and authorities in the Heavenly realms." (Ephesians 3:9-11)

- *"Oh, how great are God's riches and wisdom and knowledge! How impossible it is for us to understand His decisions and His ways!"* (Romans 11:33-36) – The secrets of the riches of His wisdom and ways of God's heart.
- *"Place me like a seal over your heart, like a seal on your arm: for love is as strong as death, its jealousy unyielding as the grave. It burns like blazing fire, like a mighty flame. Many waters cannot quench love: rivers cannot sweep it away"* (Song of Songs 8:6) – Just as Lucifer was the seal of perfection, we are to become a seal upon God's heart, and our stones are to shine, showing that His nature has been infused in us, and have become adorned on us.
- *"Store up treasures in Heaven, where moths and rust cannot destroy, and thieves do not break in and steal."* (Matthews 6:20) – As you reflect His nature, by your treasure, you reflect God's heart and what is shining in you.

Wendy Alec writes in her book *The Fall of Lucifer* – "Lucifer nodded, I was but seven moons when I walked up and down amidst the stones of fire. I could not bear to be away from Him for a moment. Lucifer stared in awe at the Stones of Fire, it is HIS PRESENCE."[8]

The Twelve Stones of Government in Heaven.

The twelve stones of fire are also connected to the everlasting government of Heaven. As one walks into the heart of God in the house of the flames of fire, one engages the twelve stones of fire. These stones contain the fullness of the DNA of God and His mysteries. As one engages them and covers them, they are baptised by fire and the stones release and infuse, via vibration and colour, the mysteries of God into that being. As this process keeps going,

---

8   Wendy Alec, *The Fall Of Lucifer*, Warboys Publishing Limited, 2005, p.119.

layers and layers of revelation are transfigured into that being, and when transformed, the likeness of that stone is adorned upon them.

As they engage the twelve stones and are transformed to the likeness of God and their function, the seal of perfection is adorned on their breastplate. From this position, one can come back and cover the stones to receive higher and deeper mysteries. This is why Lucifer was called the light bearer, he reflected the mysteries. The stones contain everlasting revelation, that is why the knowledge cannot be imparted to us by being spoken to us, for it would blow our minds to bits. For it is not by might or power, but by God's Spirit that we receive from Him. And from this baptism of fire, our spirit searches the illuminations of the Spirit in us. Through transfiguration, we are conformed into the image of God. As all Believers are seated in Heavenly places, I believe, at times, we are all engaging the stones of fire.

Lucifer was to receive nine stones, Scripture doesn't say what the twenty-four Elders were adorned with, but Adam was to go up and receive the twelve stones of the DNA of God.

Twelve is also the number of Government and Scripture says that God's Government has no end. In the stones were also the mysteries of the divine law, and Lucifer, and certain angels and the Elders were to go up and receive the mysteries of the Divine Law and bring them and reveal them in the divine councils, to debate and solve.

The setting would take place something like this, the King would walk in, that being Jesus, and take His seat on His throne, and then other thrones would come into place to set the scene of the divine council. This courtroom would be ablaze with thrones of fire and revelation, forming in books and scrolls.

> *"I watched till thrones were put in place, and the ancient of days was seated, His garment was white as snow, and the hair of his*

head was like pure wool. His throne was a fiery flame, its wheels a burning fire...the court was seated, and the books were opened." (Daniel 7:9-10)

Once the rulings were passed, the books or scrolls would be passed on to the twelve houses of Heaven, where councillors would make laws. These houses included the House of Commons, the House of Lords, the House of the Royal Courts of Justice, the House of Wisdom and so on. From here, the divine laws were administrated with resources, mandates, and treasures into the earth's atmospheres to be caught in the spirit by leaders.

You may ask, 'where do you get these twelve Heavenly houses of Governmental administration from in Scripture?' We find these houses in looking at their representatives on earth, that being, the twelve houses of the fathers of the twelve tribes.

"Thus, the children of Israel did according to all that the Lord commanded Moses, so they camped by their standards and so they broke camp, each one by his family, according to their fathers' houses." (Numbers 2:34)

The camp on earth was to be a copy of the governmental rule of Heaven above. The twelve houses were to administrate the divine laws of God into the earth.

Today we see Heaven administrating into the nations of the world by legislation and bringing kings, and governments into power to rule, and changing kings and governments in due seasons. We also see Heaven administrating through spiritual kings and lords in the Kingdom.

"Blessed be the name of God forever and ever, for wisdom and might are His. And He changes the times and the seasons, He removes kings and raises up kings, he gives wisdom to the wise

and knowledge to those who have understanding. He reveals deep and secret things, He knows what is in darkness, and light dwells with Him." (Daniel 2:20-22)

In Revelation, the Woman is the Church who gives birth to the children of God, and crowns them in likeness with a crown of twelve stars (stones):

"Now a great sign appeared in Heaven, a woman clothed with the sun, with the moon under her feet, and on her head a crown of twelve stars. Then being with child, she cried out in labour in pain to give birth." (Revelation 12:1)

To walk with governmental authority, we must engage the twelve stones of fire around the throne of God. In this engaging, our hearts are enlarged with the likeness of God, and we are transfigured into fully functioning kings and priests.

"And have made us kings and priests to our God, and we shall reign on the earth." (Revelation 5:10)

As we have seen, one of the twelve houses of governmental legislation in Heaven, which branches off from out of the DNA of the infusion of the revelation of the twelve stones of fire, is the House of wisdom.

"Wisdom is the principal thing, therefore get wisdom. And in all your getting, get understanding. Exalt her, and she will promote you; She will bring you honour when you embrace her. She will place on your head an ornament of grace; a crown of glory she will deliver to you." (Proverbs 4:7-9)

To function as a spiritual king of government, one must bath and embrace wisdom. As we engage the DNA of God's heart in the twelve stones of fire, we will be baptised by fire with an authority and function that will be recognised by the twelve stones, not only perfected on our breastplate as Sons, but also adorned in twelve stones (stars) in our crown as a king.

> *"You shall also be a crown of glory in the hand of the Lord, and a royal diadem in the hand of your God." (Isaiah 62:3)*

> *"Do you not know that those who run in a race all run, but one receives the prize? Run in such a way that you may obtain it. Everyone who competes for the prize is temperate in all things. Now they do it to obtain a perishable crown, but we for an imperishable crown." (1 Corinthians 9:24-25)*

> *"The Lord, their God, will save them in that day, as the flock of His people. For they shall be like the jewels of a crown, lifted like a banner over His land." (Zechariah 9:16)*

As we govern spiritual authority in the earth, we will be lifted up like a banner, like a standard, and be seen in the Heavens with a crown of twelve jewels.

God's heart and divine laws unfold and reveal themselves in the twelve stones of fire, to be infused into the soul, and adorned with twelves stones on our breastplate as Sons, and twelve stones in a crown as kings and fully functioning priests. Walking in the wisdom out of the twelve Heavenly houses of governmental authority, that was entrusted by the Spirit to the twelve tribes of Israel, and their twelve houses of their fathers, to govern in the earth (Numbers 2:34). The twelve tribes, the twelve apostles, the twelve foundation stones all call us to be transformed into the full nature of Christ.

There are people today, who are receiving supernatural loaves of bread with gemstones in them. You may ask, 'What does this have to do with anything?!' But as we have seen, the twelve stones of fire radiate and vibrate the presence of the DNA of God. In the wilderness, it rained down manna and precious stones, but in the tabernacle was placed twelve loaves of bread (Exodus 25). These were called the bread of His presence. As the stones of fire represent transformation, the loaves manifesting with gemstones today, are speaking of engaging the "stones of fire" in the Bread of Life, the DNA of God, of His presence.

CHAPTER FIFTEEN

Store Up Your Treasures in Your Heavenly Account

"For even while I was in Thessalonica, you provided for my needs once and again. Not that I am seeking a gift, but I am looking for the fruit that may be credited to your account. I have all I need and more, now that I have received your gifts from Epaphroditus. They are a sweet-smelling aroma, an acceptable sacrifice, well pleasing to God..." (Philippians 4:17)

"Store your treasures in Heaven, where moths and rust cannot destroy, and thieves do not break in and steal. Wherever your treasure is, there the desires of your heart will also be." (Matthews 6:20-21)

A Heavenly account? Yes, a Heavenly account, where your treasures are, and your heart needs to be.

Alfred Prempeh says in his book *Laying Up Treasures in Heaven*,

> "There is an account for you in Heaven in Christ, even as you are on earth. The moment you came into Christ, you had an account opened for you. This is a spiritual account but affects and influences one's life now in the earthly realm. It is divine and entails the totality of one's life, time, talents, and resources with their character and what they do with it on earth, as far as the kingdom of God is concerned.
>
> "The way one thinks, the way one speaks, one's way of actions and reactions to the situations and circumstances in life and one's works or deeds; all go into one's account. Whatever a person manifests, and whatever a person demonstrates, good or bad, creates an occasion and opens doors for something to be created to our account unto Him.
>
> "These can be testimonies, or a witness concerning You, in word, deeds or actions. These accounts are

credited to you in your Heavenly accounts. It also involves our lives on earth here, in relation to all what we do with our time, talents, and resources, and how it brings glory to God."[1]

In this Heavenly account, you can, by the way you live for the Kingdom of Heaven on earth, lay-up treasures for yourself in Heaven. And once created in your account, you can make withdrawals to meet every need you have in life. You do not lose your treasure, but it increases a grace for you. For if you sow, you will also reap grace with interest.

> *"Again, it will be like a man going on a journey, who called his servants and entrusted his wealth to them. To one, he gave five bags of gold, to another two bags, and to another one bag, each according to his ability. Then he went on his journey. The man who had received five bags of gold went at once and put his money to work and gained five bags more. So, also, the one with two bags of gold gained two more. But the man who had received one bag went off, dug a hole in the ground and hid his master's money. After a long time, the master of those servants returned and settled accounts with them." (Matthew 25:14-19)*

> *"Every man's work will be made clear in that day, because it will be tested by fire: and the fire itself will make clear the quality of every man's work." (1 Corinthians 3:13)*

---

[1] Alfred Prempeh-Dapaah, *Laying Up Treasures in Heaven*, Stonewall Press, 2018, p.5

The following quotes by various famous theologians are found in Bruce Wilkinson's book, *A Life God Rewards*:[2]

Martin Luther

"Now when Christ says: 'make to yourselves friends, lay up treasures, and the like', you see that He means: do good, and it will follow of itself without your seeking, that you will have friends, find treasures in Heaven, and receive a reward."

John Wesley

"God will reward everyone according to his works. But this is well consistent with his distributing advantages and opportunities for improvement, according to his own good pleasure."

John Calvin

"Nothing is clearer than that a reward is promised to good works, in order to support the weakness of our flesh by some comfort; but not to inflate our minds with vainglory."

Theodore H Epp

"The primary purpose of the Judgment Seat of Christ is the examination of the lives and service of Believers, and the rewarding of them for what God considers worthy of recognition."

---

[2] Bruce Wilkinson with David Kopp, *A Life God Rewards: Why Everything You Do Today Matters Forever*, Multnomah Publishers, Inc, 2002, p. 118-122

Johnathan Edwards

"There are many mansions in God's house because Heaven is intended for various degrees of honour and blessedness; Some are designed to sit in higher places there than others; some are designed to be advanced to higher degrees of honour and glory than others; and therefore there are various mansions, and some more honourable mansions and seats in Heaven than others. Though they are all seats of exceeding honour and blessedness, yet some more so than others."

John MacArthur JR

"There will be varying degrees of reward in Heaven. That shouldn't surprise us; there are varying degrees of giftedness even on earth."

John Wesley

"There is an inconceivable variety in the degrees of reward in the other world. Let not any slothful one say, 'If I get to Heaven at all, I will be content'."

Dwight L Moody

"If we are Christ's, we are here to shine for Him, by and by He will call us home to our reward."

Theodore H Epp

"God is eager to reward us and does everything possible to help us layup rewards. But if we are slothful and carnal, so that our service counts for nothing, we shall be saved, yet so as by fire. Let us determine by the grace of God, not to be empty-handed when we stand before the bema, the Judgment Seat of Christ."

R C Sproul

"I'd say there are at least twenty five occasions where the New Testament clearly teaches that we will be granted rewards according to our works. We are called to work, to store up treasures for ourselves in Heaven, even as the wicked, as Paul tells the Romans, 'treasure up wrath against the day of wrath'."

Billy Graham

"The believer has his foundation in Jesus Christ. Now we are to build upon this foundation, and the work we have done must stand the ultimate test; final exams come at the Judgment Seat of Christ when we receive our rewards."

Charles Stanley

"The Kingdom of God will not be the same for all Believers. Let me put it another way. Some Believers will have rewards for their earthly faithfulness; others will not. Some will reign with Christ; others will not (2 Timothy 2:12). Some will be given Heavenly treasures of their own; others will not (Luke 16:12).

Charles R Swindoll

"On top of these temporal benefits connected to serving, there are eternal rewards as well. Christ Himself, while preparing the twelve for a lifetime of serving others, promised an eternal reward even for holding out a cup of cool water."

Wayne Grudem

"It is important to realize that this judgment of Believers will be a judgment to evaluate and bestow various degrees of reward."

CHAPTER SIXTEEN

Teardrop Gemstones

Another manifestation that is occurring is the formation of "teardrop" gemstones. Every gemstone has a form and a meaning, every colour has a meaning as well. In this phenomenon, intercessors are experiencing, after great prayer battles, that little teardrop gemstones are appearing around them, as if God has seen their hearts.

Intercession is prayers that plead with God for your needs and the needs of others. Intercessory prayer takes place in the spiritual world where battles for our own lives, our families, our friends, and our nations are won or lost. You do not have to be on an intercessory team to be an intercessor. If you pray in the battles for God's heart, you are an intercessor, and in your brokenness and sorrow, the tears you weep are seen by God. For God says that He will store our tears in *skin bottles*[1] in Heaven (Psalm 56:8). As we have seen all through the previous chapters of this book, that which is in Heaven, is being shown in manifestations as a foretaste to Believers.

This is why, I believe, people are receiving teardrop gemstones. But can this be grounded in Scripture, does God's Word hint that this is possible? I would ask you to reflect on how you would interpret Psalm 56:8:

> *"You have taken account of my wonderings (Book of Remembrance). You have set (formed, and stored up) my tears in Your Skin Bottle. Are they not in Your book?"*

How do we best interpret this passage?

- ❖ It's all symbolic? It just means God knows.
- ❖ Our physical tears on earth just evaporate and appear in Heaven as water in a bottle?

---

1 Strong's Concordance, Hebrew 4997: A skin bottle, skin

❖ In remembrance of our tears of sacrifice, intercession for what is God's heart, our tears (individually) are stored up, set (formed) and put into God's Bottles?

What is more logical or Scriptural?

When it says remembered, recorded in a book, does that mean there is no physical representation? In the book of Revelation 20:12, it speaks about our works being written in a book, the book of Life. But in 1 Corinthians 3:1-15, it also speaks about our works being judged as of metals and precious stones, according to which we will be rewarded. In this context, our works are connected to a representation – Precious Stones!

Now that doesn't mean our rewards will just be precious stones, it means that there is a spiritual accounting to our account in precious stones in Him. Those metals or precious stones – may open doors to greater glories and gifts in Heaven. We will have to wait and see when that glorious day comes.

If our prayers are a spiritual work, which they are, is it impossible that our tears may be "formed" in "teardrop" gemstones and manifest as a foretaste or a sign that God has seen our tears?

Or are we to believe that the passage just means, God knows we are crying, and in His creativity of wonder, He just ticks a box in Heaven. I believe it means more, and the fact is, these stones are manifesting around intercessors.

The word "Skin Bottle" in Psalm 56:8 may even be speaking of being in God's human flesh. Teardrop gemstones might manifest on earth, they might get formed and set in bottles in Heaven, as a beautiful remembrance of the treasure of sacrificial love in a saint's heart, flowing out in their tears while on earth, or they might even be studded in the flesh of Jesus,

> "His arms are rods of gold adorned with gems; His loins, a work of ivory covered with sapphires. His legs, pillars of alabaster, resting on golden pedestals. His appearance, like the Lebanon, imposing as the cedars. His mouth is sweetness itself; He is delightful in every way. Such is my lover, and such my friend, Daughters of Jerusalem." (Song of Songs 5:14-16)

In the book, *Talk With Me in Paradise*, Angela Curtis, writing about a personal friend of mine's Heavenly encounter, reveals there is a "Pool of Tears",

> "I have seen the place where our tears have been collected in reflecting glass jars of all sizes. The Lord takes me there when He wants me to sit and listen to what's on His heart. I've been there numerous times when I was concerned about someone at the campus. Sometimes, He shows me a bottle and tells me why they were shed. We pray together over the situation, and He sends His angels to answer the person's prayers. There is a huge body of water, like a lake, that is called the 'tears pool'. It is where our tears are collected when we cry out to God in intercession for others. The angels told me that Jesus' tears are also in this pool. They are added when He walks through valleys by our side and cries with us. Jesus taught me how the tears in the bottles are incredibly powerful, how they are used by the angels for spiritual warfare, and how some turn into extraordinary gems after our prayers have been answered. Those sparkling gems are placed into a special wall so exquisite; I couldn't help but be moved. Especially knowing these tears have come from someone weeping in pain. I will never think negatively about my tears again."[2]

---

[2] Angela Curtis, *Talk With Me in Paradise*, Kin & Kingdom Book, 2019 p. 121

Wendy Alec, in her book *Visions of Heaven*, reveals these same glass canisters of tears in her heavenly encounter. She writes,

> "The Father picked up the most exquisitely cut glass canister filled to the brim with liquid. 'These are your tears that you shed during your time of intense trial.' He picked up another much, much larger canister. 'And, these are the tears that I shed, For you.' And the Father lifted the canister of His tears and poured them over the blood seeping from my heart. Instantly the blood stopped flowing, and a great comfort washed over my heart."[3]

The God of love and compassion is revealed. Jewish tradition says, at times (Jesus) weeps with us in Heaven, as we walk through trials on earth. *"In all their troubles, He was troubled (moved)"* (Isaiah 63:9).

Rabbi Kalonymus Shapira says that God weeps in His innermost chamber:

> *"For if you will not heed, My inmost self must weep in secret, because of your arrogance." (Jeremiah 13:17a)*

God goes on to say,

> *"My eyes will weep bitterly and run down with tears, because the Lord's flock has been taken captive." (Jeremiah 13:17b)*

B. Berakhot 59a says that God's tears flow down His fingers into an ocean pool that builds spiritual power to be released on the earth. Is this a contradiction to Revelation 21:4 of no tears or crying? No, as that is when Heaven is on earth, and all things are restored. The atmosphere of Heaven is not sad or in pain, but in comfort and perfect love, yet there is emotion until that day,

---

3 Wendy Alec, *Visions of Heaven*, Warboys Publishing, 2013, P. 25.

carrying the saints along on earth. God's emotion is not a weakness, and His perfect strength keeps Him from breaking, and His wisdom conquers, and His heart wins.

"Jesus wept. Then the Jews said, see how He loved him!"
(John 11:35)

The Wall in Heaven with the gems of precious stones in the shape of tears, is the Heavenly copy of the "Wailing Wall" of the Temple on earth. Jewish tradition says that every morning, drops of dew can be seen on its stones, and it was said that at night the Wall was crying for the Temple (Believers are the Temple, Living Stones). They say women collected the tears of the Wall as precious remedies for many ailments, spiritual remedies.

CHAPTER SEVENTEEN

Multi-dimensional Revelation Stones of Glory!

In this Chapter, I would like to show that the precious stones were adorned on the outside and inside of the Temples. The word "Temple" in Scripture is multi-dimensional and speaks of many categories as one. Temples, Gardens, Tents, and Brides are spoken of in Scripture as representing physical buildings and also Believers. This is a kind of typology, the study of classification based on types or categories. Therefore, Scripture can talk of a believer as a Temple, Garden, a Tent and also a Bride, in the sense that the Tabernacles were known as being a Bride.

> In 1 Kings 7:9, it says that the Temple was fitted with precious stones on the inside and outside, and 2 Chronicles 3:6 says,
>
> *"Further he adorned the house with precious stones; and the gold was gold from Parvaim."*

These two verses reveal to us that the Temple was adorned. We will first look at the adorning on the outside of the Temple, adorned in the sense that precious stones fell in the wilderness (Tabernacle) and in the sense that white marble and gold covered the second Temple. Marble is considered a semi-precious stone. Josephus said,

> "But this Temple appeared as they approached, it seemed in the distance like a mountain covered with snow; for any part not covered with gold was dazzling white."[1]

The precious stones were also inside the Tabernacle and Temple. In the furnishing, in the utensils, and in the treasury.

The functions of priests, lords, and kings also speak of Believers who experience being adorned on the outside. And they can also have precious stones on the inside that come out of their human flesh (yes, this happens). Because the kingdom is within us, many Believers are experiencing that stones can supernaturally come out

---

1 Josephus, The Wars of the Jews 5, p.223

their hands and body parts. The Kingdom can manifest around us and out of us, both adorning us.

Having read previous chapters, stop and reflect on each reference on how the precious stones are on the outside and inside of the categories mentioned. Precious stones manifest around these categories. Read as a building and as a Believer!

- Don't you know *you* are a Temple? (1 Corinthians 3:16)
- Don't you know *you* are a Bride? And the Bride was also a Temple (Song of Songs 1:5)
- The stones were fitted "on" the outside and "in" the inside. (1 Kings 7:9)
- The stones were "adorned", and the stones were held in the secret place inside the Temple – "kingdom" within. (Exodus 25:16)
- The stones overshadowed on the outside (fell in the wilderness, and were placed in the walls of the tabernacle) "Then the cloud covered the tabernacle of meeting, and the glory of the Lord filled the tabernacle" (Exodus 40:34) and the stones that fell, were placed in the inside of the Temple as in the utensils, and stones in the ark. (the Kingdom within - 1 Kings 7:9) So we see – the stones overshadowed…were used on the outside and in the inside of the Temples (the Kingdom within).
- The City and Temple above can adorn as it comes down (Revelation 21:2) – And the Temple on earth can be adorned as we tabernacle (as we live in our temples) in our bodies.
- The stones are "on" (adorn) the Priests, Brides, Lords, and Kings. The Lord was the husband of the Bride, so He also had his precious stones (Isaiah 54:5).
- The stones adorned the Bride, in engagement, and as gifts, and as she was lead to the Father's house (journey of life), and also once in the Father's house (married as a couple). (John 14:2 and Isaiah 61:10)

- ❖ The stones are "in" the Tent, Temples, Garden, Living stones, Gates, and Heart.
- ❖ The Garden of Eden was known as a Sanctuary and as a Temple. (Ezekiel 28:18) – The Garden of God, in which Lucifer walked, and which verse 18 says he defiled his sanctuaries. Every temple in scripture was inscribed with garden plants, referring back to the Garden.
- ❖ We are a Garden – the bride is a garden locked up (Song of Songs 4:12). We are an Eden, where the river of God was full of stones (Genesis 2:12). – Our souls are like a Garden -"You shall be a watered garden a spring of water who waters don't fail." (Isaiah 58:11) – Wonder why stones come out of people?
- ❖ You are a child of God, the stones on the breastplates spoke of all the children of God in Heavenly realms, as the Priests garments represented the cosmos. The cosmos was considered a Temple and a Bride as in the Creation Covenant. Therefore, stones can fall around us and on us, and come out of us for we are part of creation.
- ❖ You are a Daughter of Zion, the City that God promised to rebuild with precious stones (Isaiah 54:11-12)
- ❖ You are a "Gate" – *"Lift up your heads, you everlasting gates."* (Psalms 24:7). The gates had precious stones, on the earthly Temple (Jesus is the Temple, John 10:7 – Song of Songs 5:14-16) and Heavenly (Revelation 21:21).
- ❖ The forty days and forty nights of Jesus' temptations in the wilderness echo Israel's forty years in the wilderness. Jesus is the true Israel and true Temple, of which we are a Temple in a Temple, a gateway, through the door, with Jesus being adorned with precious stones.
- ❖ Out of your hearts flow treasures (stones), for where your heart is, your treasure is also. (Matthew 6:21)
- ❖ You are a "Living Stone" in the Temple (1 Peter 2:5), and you can give birth to stones (children) – physically, spiritually and with Jewels.

- ❖ The Lord promises "I will give you hidden treasures, riches stored in secret places, so that you may know that I AM the Lord, the God of Israel, who summons you by name." (Isaiah 45:3)
- ❖ The stones are "multi-dimensional" revelation stones because they speak of the perfect Rock and His glory and love – God reflecting through us. Even Jesus is studded with precious stones (Song of Songs 5:14-16). Were they placed on him, or did they come out of him?
- ❖ Faith is a substance – Let's get real people! Was the manna, the multiplying of bread, precious stones falling, and miracles in the Bible just symbols or reality?

God will adorn with multi-dimensions those who believe.

CHAPTER EIGHTEEN

Eden, Garden, Tabernacle in the Wilderness, and the Church

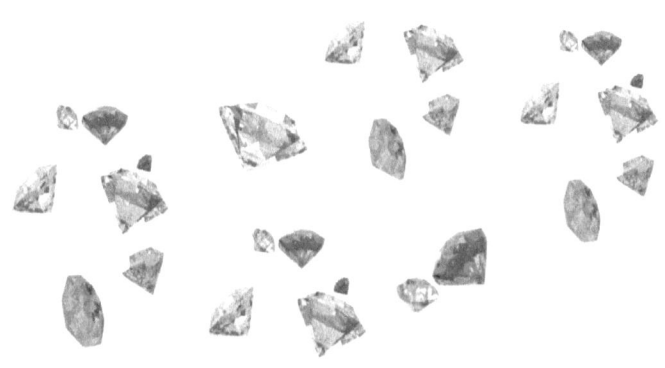

"For the Lord will comfort Zion, He will comfort all her waste places. He will make her wilderness like Eden, And her desert like the garden of the Lord." (Isaiah 51:3)

There is a pattern flowing from the Throne of God through Eden, the Garden, the Tabernacle, and the Church. Before we look at this pattern, the first question we need to answer is, "Who is 'her' in Isaiah 51:3?" The answer to this question is "Israel", the children of God, His bride. The 'her' in this passage is God speaking of His people as His bride.

"The word of the Lord came to me, saying, 'Go and proclaim in the hearing of Jerusalem, saying, Thus says the LORD: 'I remember the devotion of your youth, your love as a bride, how you followed me in the wilderness, in a land not sown.' Israel was holy to the LORD, the first fruits of his harvest." (Jeremiah 2:1-3)

Rabbi Jose, says that "The Lord came from Sinai, to receive Israel, as a bridegroom comes forth to meet the bride." (Mekilta on Exodus 19:17).

As we have seen, God's people were viewed as the bride; the temple itself also represented the bride.

In the book of Song of Songs, the bride's body resembles the land of Israel, and her appearance and fragrances resembled the temple. In the Songs, the tents of Kedar are dark and tanned (like the wilderness Tabernacle) and beautiful like the curtains of Solomon (1:5). The Temple was built based on the movement of the sun, and so with each sunrise, the Temple looked as though it were being "dressed" in fine white garments.[1]

We see how beautifully the tabernacle resembles the bride in the wilderness, and how the temple resembles the bride. God's presence lived in both, pointing to Jesus. Jesus said that He was the true temple, and in the tabernacle and temple, we see the union of the bride and bridegroom as one, the two living as one.

Isaiah 51:3 also says God will make her like Eden, and her desert like the garden of the Lord. This passage is saying there is going to be some demonstration that in the wilderness experience, it is going to look in characteristics like Eden and capture the idea of the garden of the Lord.

Let's go to Eden,

> *"Now a river flowed out of Eden to water the garden." (Genesis 2:10-14)*

Carl Callups says in his book, *Gods of Ground Zero: The Truth of Eden's Iniquity*,

> "Sometimes 'Eden' and the 'Garden of Eden' are used synonymously. However, they are not the same. Eden was an entire region of the newly created planet, while the 'Garden of Eden' was located within that region. The Talmudic and Midrash sources know of two Gardens of Eden; the terrestrial, of abundant fertility and vegetation, and the celestial, which serves as the habitation of souls of the righteous."[2]

---

[1] Dinah Dye, *The Temple Revealed in Creation: A Portrait Of The Family*, Foundations of Torah Publishers, 2016, p.181.

[2] Carl Gallups, *Gods of Ground Zero, The Truth of Eden's Iniquity*, Defender Publishing, 2018, p.37

Eden is God's garden, but God planted another garden eastwards, that being Adam's garden (Genesis 2:8). Adam's garden was separated from Eden but was joined in the sense that an open portal over the garden gave access to Adam and Eve to go up into Eden. The gardens were spiritually joined and overlaid each other. Therefore, the text reads "God planted a garden eastward in Eden." Gardens were symbolic of Temples, and Eden is God's mountain Temple, and the garden was Adam's Temple.

From God's throne on the mountain, flows living water, a fountain (Jeremiah 17:12-14). This fountain flows into a river, a crystal river (Revelation 22:1). The Hebrew word for "River" is "Nahar". It comes from the root verb Nahar meaning to shine, beam, light, burn, be radiant, to flow.[3]

Eden was above, the garden of Adam's was below on earth. In Gen 1:2 – the Spirit of God was hovering and moving upon the waters. The Heavenly veil that separated Eden from the garden sanctuary was likened to the "firmament". In the Tabernacle, a curtain of blue, scarlet, purple of fine white linen, woven with cherubim, separated the holy of holies (Eden) from the holy place (garden).

The river of life shines light like a crystal, for it is full of precious stones. From Eden (above) the crystal river flows and divides, and four springs flow through the veil into Adam's garden.

> *"For the lamb at the centre of the throne will be their Shepard; He will lead them to springs of living water." (Revelation 7:17)*

The river which flows out of Eden, is both fire and water and is consumed with the Holy Spirit's presence.

One of the divided rivers is named "Pishon", and it flows through the whole land of Havilah, where there is Gold, Bdellium

---

[3] Strongs Concordance 5102: https://biblehub.com/str/hebrew/5102.htm

& Onyx. The word "Pishon" means to increase and spread out, and the word "Havilah" means to "travail", like birth pangs and tribulation. The gold there, symbolizes the garden state of innocence and pureness. Therefore, the garden is an ever-increasing womb of innocence. The Septuagint calls the Bdellium a crystal stone. The crystal is able to take the white light of the river and separate it into the seven colours of the rainbow. The "Pishon" river was not a little stream, but a burning, radiant river, shining out the colours of the rainbow up and over the garden (Adams Temple) like a canopy. This manifestation is very much like the rainbow that shines over God's throne in Eden. (Revelation 4:3)

In the river is where the Onyx stones were. The Onyx stone is normally black, but the word Onyx comes from the word "Shoham", which means "to make white".[4] Spiritually speaking, we call this process sanctification or holiness. The Onyx stones were on the High Priest's shoulders with the names of the twelve tribes of Israel. The Onyx stones represented the state of holy transparency.[5]

Genesis 2:9 says that a mist went up from the earth and watered the whole face of the ground. This mist came from the four rivers, the presence of God's Spirit, in the water of life, ascending up to water the earth in the garden with life.

SO, WHAT DOES THIS HAVE TO DO WITH THE WILDERNESS?

God had His Eden (above), Adam had his garden and Temple (on earth). The Jews believed that the fact of creation, the separating of the Heavens and earth and them re-joining in the future as one, is God marrying His bride of creation. As Heaven

---

4 Strong's Hebrew: 7718; http://biblehub.net/searchhebrew.php?q=shoham
5 K. Gallagher, The Rivers of Eden. (Oct 2014).   https://graceintorah.net/2014/10/17/ the-rivers-of-eden/

was full of precious stones, they also were to adorn creation. For the stones would come down in the spirit, the river, through the veil.

Israel had its Tabernacle on earth. Israel's Tabernacle/Temple was to be like Eden, being the garden in Eden. The children of God and the Temples were known as brides. And as Heaven is full of precious stones, the children of God and the Temples were/are to be adorned with precious stones.

> *"O generation, see the word of the Lord! Have I been a wilderness to Israel, Or a land of darkness?... Can a virgin forget her ornaments, Or a bride her attire, yet My people have forgotten Me days without number." (Jeremiah 2:31-32)*

The land Havilah meant travail and tribulation, and we know Israel walked through the land of tribulation. The river "Pishon," which flowed out of Heaven through the veil of separation, through the garden/land, meant increase, and spread out. This river, the spirit of life, was to increase and spread Israel out and give them life. As Heaven was full of precious stones, and Israel was to be like Eden, the Spirit of God dropped manna and precious stones in the wilderness. The desert was to be like the garden of the Lord, stones were in the river, and the bread of God's presence was in the garden too, which would be over the Tabernacle/Temple, bride as well. As the Tabernacle/Temple was seen as a bride, it was covered inside and out with precious stones. The gold in Heaven, the garden and in the Temples and on the brides of Israel's fingers, represented the pureness of God.

When it says in Genesis 2:9, *"a mist went up from the earth"*, it is talking about the dew from the river of life, God's Spirit. As the Pishon river had Bdellium and Onyx stones in it, in the garden, and as God's Spirit came down again to water (coming first from the Throne), it rained spiritually on Israel through the firmament for 40 years with manna and precious stones. These precious stones shone the light of the glory of God (*"Like the appearance of a rainbow in the clouds on a rainy day, so was the radiance around Him. This was the appearance of the likeness of the glory of the Lord"* – Ezekiel 1:28). The gold, the precious stones, and the manna were to be in the desert – in the "Land" (garden), the "Temple" and on and around the "Bride".

> *"Now the manna was like coriander, and its colour like the bdellium." (Numbers 11:7).*

This is why the Rabbis say precious stones fell in the wilderness with the manna, for the wilderness was to be like Eden.

The Church today, is also called the bride, and each believer is also a temple and a garden. So, if we are to follow the pattern, precious stones will adorn the "Church", His "Temple", and the "Bride".

> *"For he has clothed me with the garments of salvation, He has covered me with the robe of righteousness, as a bridegroom decks himself with ornaments, and as a bride adorns herself with her jewels." (Isaiah 61:10)*

If Heaven is to manifest on earth, then we should be open to receiving physical substance. For faith is the substance of things hoped for, the evidence of things not seen (Hebrews 11:1). This means there are evidences of another world not seen yet, that can appear. This is why our hearts cry should be *"Your kingdom come, Your will be done, On earth as it is in Heaven."* (Matthew 6:10)

If creation is to be married as a bride when Heaven comes to earth, will not God adorn His creation? Could not precious stones manifest from Heaven to adorn creation, and also His sons and daughters as the bride of Christ? As Christ's return gets closer and the wedding day comes near, we will see more manifestations. Manna is manifesting in some places of the world. 'Why?' you may ask. Because, at weddings, special bread was eaten. Water is also turning into wine at a few places I know. Again, this was a sign that a wedding was near (John 2:1-11).

In early Christianity, Baptism was a sign of a bridal bath…Is this not another reason why God can adorn us with gifts?

Brant Pitre, in his book called *Jesus the Bridegroom*, says:

> "In both Jewish and Greek cultures of that time, the immediate cosmetic preparation of the bride included a bath with fragrant oils so that she could be as clean and beautiful as possible. Baptism, Paul is saying, is the Church's bridal bath that prepares her to be united to her bridegroom".

You may question the above statement. Brant is a well-known scholar who interprets customs. Admittedly, according to Romans 6:4 and Colossians 2:12, Paul is speaking of a spiritual *burial and resurrection*, but he's giving deeper meaning to what was understood of baptism – which was also believed to be a "bath to cleanse from sins," just as Bride has her preparatory bath.

> *"Husbands, love your wives, as Christ loved the Church and gave himself up for her, that he might sanctify her, having cleansed her by the washing of water with the Word, that he might present the Church to himself in splendour, without spot or wrinkle or any such thing, that she might be holy and without blemish."*
> *(Ephesians 5:25-27)*

An online Dictionary says of the word 'Splendour" – Splendour is defined as great brilliance, richness or glory. An example of Splendour is an elegantly decorated wedding reception hall.

CHAPTER NINETEEN

The Full Council of Scripture

Jesus is the eternal stone: Jasper, Sardius, Cornerstone, Capstone

1. *"And He who sat there was like a Jasper and Sardius stone in appearance, and there was a rainbow around the throne, in appearance like an emerald." (Revelation 4:3)*
2. *"Therefore, thus says the Lord God, Behold, I lay in Zion a stone for a foundation. A tried stone, a precious cornerstone, a sure foundation." (Isaiah 28:16)*
3. *"And he shall bring forth the capstone with shouts of 'grace, grace' to it." (Zecheriah 4:7).*
4. *"His hands are rods of gold, set with beryl. His body is carved ivory inlaid with sapphires. His legs are pillars of marble set on bases of fine gold." (Song of Songs 5:14)*

Jesus, the eternal stone sits on a Sapphire Throne.

5. *"And I looked. And there in the firmament that was above the head of the cherubim there appeared something like a sapphire stone, having the appearance of the likeness of a throne." (Ezekiel 10:1)*
6. *"And He showed me a pure river of water of life, clear as crystal, proceeding from the throne of God and of the Lamb." (Revelation 22:1)*

A rainbow shines over the Throne reflecting seven stones: Ruby – red; Jacinth – orange; Topaz -yellow; Emerald – green; Chalcedony – blue; Sapphire – indigo; Amethyst – violet.

7. *"Like the appearance of a rainbow in a cloud on a rainy day, so was the appearance of the brightness all around it. This was the appearance of the likeness of the Lord." (Ezekiel 1:28)*

In God, there is the breath of life, the spirit of wisdom, perfection, and knowledge; the eternal stone shines forth His Spirit.

8. *"The Mighty One, God the Lord, has spoken and called the earth from the rising of the sun to its going down. Out of Zion, the perfection of*

beauty, God will shine forth, and shall not keep silent. A fire shall devour before Him, and it shall be very tempestuous all around Him." (Psalms 50:1-3)
9. *"For the Lord gives Wisdom, from His mouth come knowledge and understanding." (Proverbs 2:6)*
10. *"But we speak the wisdom of God in a mystery, the hidden mystery which God ordained before the ages for our glory." (1 Corinthians 2:7)*

In the eternal stone, that being Jesus, there was from the foundation of the world, treasure hidden in Him.

11. *"In Christ Jesus is hidden all the treasures of wisdom and knowledge" (Colossians 2:3)*
12. *"Just as He chose us in Him before the foundation of the world, that we should be holy…" (Ephesians 1:4)*
13. *"For every good gift and every perfect gift is from above and comes down from the Father of Lights with whom there is no variation or shadow of turning. Of His own will He brought us forth by the word of truth, that we might be a kind of first fruit of His creatures." (James 1:17-18)*
14. *"Coming to Him as to a living stone rejected indeed by men, but chosen by God and precious, you also, as living stones, are being built up a spiritual house, a holy priesthood, to offer up spiritual sacrifices acceptable to God through Jesus Christ." (1 Peter 2:4-5)*

The eternal mystery of the ages was that in God, His living stones would be chosen and predestined from the foundation of the world to reflect the nature of God going from glory to glory. In God, His light, His presence shines the fullness of wisdom through His living stones, and as they reflect like precious stones, the fullness of wisdom, beauty, and knowledge is revealed to the universe. In fact, the mystery was to show forth this truth to the principalities and powers in the Heavenly places.

> *"And to make all see what is the fellowship of the mystery, which from the beginning of the ages has been hidden in God, who created all things through Jesus Christ, to the intent that now the manifold wisdom of God might be made known by the church to the principalities and powers in the Heavenly places according to the eternal purpose which he accomplished in Christ Jesus our Lord." (Ephesians 3:9-11)*

Before the Throne, are the seven spirits of God that manifest various facets of wisdom and revelation.

> 15. *"The Spirit of the Lord will rest on him, the spirit of wisdom and understanding, the spirit of counsel and strength, the spirit of knowledge and the fear of the Lord." (Isaiah 11:2)*
> 16. *"Grace to you and peace from Him who is and who was and who is to come, and from the seven spirits who are before His throne." (Revelation 1:4)*

There is also a correlation between the nine spiritual gifts and the seven spirits of God: Word of Wisdom, Word of Knowledge, Discerning of Spirits, Tongues, Interpretation of Tongues, Prophecy, Faith, Working of Miracles, and Gifts of Healing.

Over the Throne, there was the anointed cherub who covered God's presence. Lucifer was able to look into God and see the one "who is and who was and who is to come".

> 17. *"You were the anointed cherub who covers, I established you. You were on the holy mountain of God, You walked back and forth in the midst of fiery stones." (Ezekiel 28:14)*
> 18. *"Grace to you and peace from Him who is and who was and who is to come, and from the seven Spirits who are before His throne." (Revelation 1:4)*

Lucifer had the seal of perfection, beauty, and wisdom because he covered the full presence of God. As Lucifer walked amidst the stones of fire in the heart of God, the stones vibrated the secrets of God's nature, and these shone into Lucifer. As Lucifer yielded his heart into God's heart, and these secrets were infused into him, precious stones were placed into Lucifer's breastplate as a seal of perfection.

> 19. *"You were the seal of perfection, full of wisdom and perfect in beauty. You were in Eden, the garden of God. Every precious stone was your covering, the sardius, topaz, and diamond, beryl, onyx, and jasper, sapphire, turquoise, and emerald with gold." (Ezekiel 28:13)*
> 20. *"Out of Zion, the perfection of beauty, God will shine forth, and shall not keep silent. A fire shall devour before Him, and it shall be very tempestuous all around Him." (Psalms 50:1-3)*

Lucifer covered the Throne of God and His presence, and I believe he also saw Believers in God's heartbeat. Lucifer got his perfection and beauty from reflecting God's presence, and was constructed inwardly so that his very breathing produced music (like pipes) (Ezekiel 28:13) as he yielded to the breath of God. He also covered in the sense of having nine precious stones on him, which filtered the revelation of God's glory throughout the heavens.

Lucifer had nine precious stones upon him, covering stones, these were to reflect the manifold wisdom of God and the nine gifts of the spirit.

> 21. *"Every precious stone was your covering, the sardius, topaz, and diamond, beryl, onyx, and jasper, Sapphire, turquoise, and emerald with gold." (Ezekiel 28:13)*

Once Lucifer had seen the mystery of the ages in God, that it would be Believers who would shine forth the manifold fullness of God's image, he became corrupt, and jealousy rose in his heart that mankind would be greater than his image. So, he set out to set himself up as God and went out to trade us, living stones to be his.

In this battle, he rebelled in his heart and took a third of the angels with him, and God threw him out of Heaven. Lucifer could not stand the concept that a people would shine forth in the beauty of grace and perfection.

Because of Lucifer's heart and hatred, the Jewels (Believers) are at the centre of cosmic conflict. From the very beginning, Lucifer's heart has been to trade us, to own us, and use our gifts to be used for himself and our destruction.

22. *"By the abundance of your trading, you became filled with violence within, and you sinned. Therefore, I cast you as a profane thing out of the mountain of God, and I destroyed you, O covering cherub, from the midst of the fiery stones. Your heart was lifted up because of your beauty, You corrupted your wisdom for the sake of your splendour." (Ezekiel 28:16-17)*
23. *"You surely shall not die! For God knows that in the day you eat from it, your eyes will be opened, and you will be like God, knowing good and evil." (Genesis 3:4-5)*
24. *"Then Jesus was led up by the Spirit into the wilderness to be tempted by the devil." (Matthew 4:1)*
25. *"Be sober, be vigilant, because your adversary, the devil, walks about like a roaring lion, seeking whom he may devour." (1 Peter 5:8)*

Every garden was a Temple, and every Temple was a house for God. We see this in God's Garden, in Eden's Garden, in the Old Testament Temples, and in the Church's spiritual Temple.

26. *"Who serve the copy and shadow of the Heavenly things, as Moses was divinely instructed when he was about to make the tabernacle. For he said, 'See that you make all things according to the pattern shown you on the mountain'." (Hebrews 8:5)*
27. *"The Lord God planted a garden eastward in Eden, and there He put the man whom He formed." (Genesis 2:8)*
28. *"You shall be like a well-watered garden, and like a spring of water, whose waters do not fail." (Isaiah 58:11)*

29. *"In whom the whole building, being fitted together, grows into a holy temple in the Lord, in whom you also are being built together for a dwelling place of God in the Spirit." (Ephesians 2:21-22)*
30. *"Do you not know that you are the temple of God and that the Spirit of God dwells in you?" (1 Corinthians 3:16)*

The stones were in all gardens and temples to remind us "who" we came out of (God), and of our value, worth, and reflection.

31. *"You were the anointed cherub who covers, I established you. You were on the holy mountain of God, You walked back and forth in the midst of fiery stones." (Ezekiel 28:14)*
32. *"Now a river went out of Eden…And the gold of that land is good. Bdellium and the onyx stone are there." (Genesis 2:10,12)*
33. *"For the Lord will comfort Zion, He will comfort all her waste places, He will make her wilderness like Eden, and her desert like the garden of the Lord." (Isaiah 51:3)*
34. *"Now the manna was like coriander seed, and its colour like the colour of bdellium stone." (Numbers 11:7)*
35. *"Now for the house of my God I have prepared with all my might: gold for things to be made of gold, silver for the things of silver, bronze for things of bronze, iron for things of iron, wood for things of wood, onyx stones, and stones to be set, glistening stones of various colours, all kinds of precious stones, and marble slabs in abundance." (1 Chronicles 29:2)*
36. *"Coming to Him as to a living stone rejected indeed by men, but chosen by God and precious, you also, as living stones, are being built up a spiritual house, a holy priesthood, to offer up spiritual sacrifices acceptable to God through Jesus Christ." (1 Peter 2:4-5)*

These stones are a revelation to remind us of our "image" – "For since the creation of the world His invisible attributes are clearly seen, being understood by the things that are made, even His eternal power and Godhead, so that they are without excuse." (Romans 1:20)

Our human body is a Temple and houses a Jewel (our spirit), and when we come into God's glory, gold can manifest from out of our pores, just like the physical Temples were covered with gold. Scripture speaks of our bodies as golden bowls.

> 37. *"Remember Him, before the silver cord is broken, and the golden bowl is crushed, the pitcher by the wall is shattered, and the wheel at the cistern is crushed; then the dust will return to the earth as it was, and the spirit will return to God who gave it." (Ecclesiastes 12:6-7)*

Silver not only speaks of our spirit, but silver was also used as mortar to cement the stones of the physical Temple together. Then the whole house (Temple) was overlaid with gold and garnished with precious stones for beauty. "The larger room he panelled with cypress which he overlaid with fine gold, and he carved palm trees and chain work on it. And he decorated the house with precious stones for beauty, and the gold was gold from Parvaim." (2 Chronicles 3:6-7)

As the pillars in the Temples were covered with gold, gold can manifest on us as we become pillars in the Temple.

> 38. *"You shall hang it upon the four pillars of acacia wood overlaid with gold. Their hooks shall be gold, upon four sockets of silver." (Exodus 26:32)*
> 39. *"And when James, Cephus, and John who seemed to be pillars..." (Galatians 2:9)*
> 40. *"He who overcomes, I will make him a pillar in the temple of My God..." (Revelation 3:12)*

As the physical Temples were decked with precious stones, so does God deck His bride, His people with precious stones in their hands or around them. He adorns them!

> 41. *"For He has clothed me with the garments of salvation, He has covered me with the robe of righteousness. As a Bridegroom decks himself with ornaments, and as a bride adorns herself with jewels. For the earth*

brings forth its bud, as the garden causes the things that are sown in it to spring forth." (Isaiah 61:10)
42. *"O generation, see the word of the Lord. Have I been a wilderness to Israel or a land of darkness? Why do My people say, We are lords, We will come no more to You? Can a virgin forget her ornaments or a bride her attire? Yet My people have forgotten Me days without number." (Jeremiah 2:31-32)*
43. *"I will give you the treasures of darkness. And hidden riches of secret places, that you may know that I, the Lord, who call you by name, I Am the God of Israel." (Isaiah 45:3)*
44. *"And I will give him a white stone, and on the stone, a new name written which no one knows except him who receives it." (Revelation 2:17)*

As the Heavenly Temple is also spoken of as a Bride, as this spiritual Temple overshadows us, this being when the kingdom of Heaven breaks into our realm, manifesting the atmosphere of Heaven, precious stones can and will manifest.

45. *"Then I John, saw the holy city, New Jerusalem, coming down from Heaven from God, prepared as a bride adorned for her husband. And I heard a loud voice from Heaven saying, behold, the tabernacle of God is with men, and He will dwell with them, and they shall be His people. God, Himself will be with them and be their God." (Revelation 21:2-3)*

As the Bride of Christ, we are also Holy Priests. And as the Priests of old had precious stones adorned on them, we should expect them to be in our lives too.

46. *"And these are the garments which they shall make, an ephod, a robe, a skilfully woven tunic, a turban, and a sash. So, they shall make holy garments for Aaron, your brother and his sons, that he may minister to Me as priest." (Exodus 28:4)*
47. *"You shall make the breastplate of judgement...And you shall put settings of stones in it, four rows of stones. The first row shall be a*

sardius, a topaz, and an emerald; this shall be the first row, the second row shall be a turquoise, a sapphire, and a diamond, the third row, a jacinth, an agate, and an amethyst, and the fourth row, a beryl, an onyx, and a jasper. They shall be set in gold settings." (Exodus 28:15; 17-20)

48. "And you shall put in the breastplate of judgment the Urim and the Thummim, and they shall be over Aarons' heart when he goes in before the Lord." (Exodus 28:30)

49. "But you are a chosen generation, a royal priesthood, a holy nation, His own special people, that you may proclaim the praises of Him who called you out of darkness into His marvellous light" (1 Peter 2:9)

We are also Kings in Christ as well as a Bride and a Priest.

50. "Then David took their king's crown from his head, and found it to weigh a talent of gold, and there were precious stones in it. And it was set on David's head." (1 Chronicles 20:2)

51. "The king made a great throne of ivory..." and "was covered with precious stones and jewels." (1 Kings 10:18)

52. "To Him who loved us and washed us from our sins in His own blood, and has made us kings and priests to His God and Father, to Him be glory and dominion forever and ever. Amen." (Revelation 1:5,6)

53. "For You [Jesus] were slain, and have redeemed us to God by Your blood out of every tribe and tongue and people and nation, and have made us kings and priests to our God; and we shall reign on the earth." Revelation 5:9b,10)

As we were placed in Christ's breastplate (heart) before the foundation of the world as a hidden treasure, so too, were stones hidden in the breastplate of the Priest, which he wore over his heart. We are in Him, and He is in us. These two stones, the "Urim" and the "Thummim" were used for divine revelation.

54. "In Christ Jesus is hidden all the treasures of wisdom and knowledge" (Colossians 2:3)

Inside the breastplate, there was a little pocket called 'chosen' where Urim and Thummim were placed. The Urim (Lights) and Thummim (Perfection) hidden in the ephod of the high priest bearing the twelve precious stones of the tribes of Israel represent Jesus Christ hidden within the lineage of the Israelites. Jesus the Urim (Lights) and Thummim (Perfection); within Him, is hidden the wisdom of God and all the children of God.

Scripture says that physical and spiritual stones will cry out, giving revelation.

> 55. *"But He answered and said to them, I tell you that if these should keep silent, the stones would immediately cry out." (Luke 19:40)*
> 56. *"For the stones will cry out from the wall, and the beams from the timbers will echo it." (Habakkuk 2:11)*
> 57. *"You will arise and have mercy on Zion: For the time to favour her, Yes, the set time has come. For your servants take pleasure in her stones, and show favour to her dust." (Psalms 102:13-14)*
> 58. *"Go through the gates! Prepare the way for the people, build up, build up the highway. Take out the stones; lift up a banner for the peoples." (Isaiah 62:10)*
> 59. *"Their heart cried out to the Lord, O wall of the daughter of Zion, Let tears run down like a river day and night…" (Lamentations 2:18)*
> 60. *"And they cried with a loud voice, saying, How Long, O Lord, holy and true, until you judge and avenge our blood on those who dwell on the earth." (Revelation 6:10)*

Because our spirit is a Jewel, our spiritual works will be judged according to different "glories" of precious metals and precious stones.

> 61. *"Now if anyone builds on this foundation with gold, silver, precious stones, wood, hay or straw, each one's work will become clear, for the day will declare it, because it will be revealed by fire, and the fire will test each one's work, of what sort it is. If anyone's work which he has built on ensures, he will receive a reward. If anyone's work is burned, he will suffer loss, but himself will be saved, yet so as through fire." (1 Corinthians 3:12-15)*

62. *"Look to yourselves, that we do not lose those things we have worked for, but that we may receive a full reward." (2 John 1:8)*

It was believed that above the holy of holies, was located the treasury of the kingdom. The word 'treasuries' means 'wealth stored up'. Polished and Glorified spirits are Jewels that will live in the presence of God.

63. *"For they shall be like the jewels of a crown, lifted like a banner over His land." (Zechariah 9:16)*
64. *"They shall be mine, says the Lord of hosts, On the day that I make them My jewels, And I will spare them, as a man spares his own son who serves him." (Malachi 3:17)*
65. *"But lay up for yourselves treasures in Heaven, where neither moth nor rust destroys and where thieves do not break in and steal. For where your treasure is, there your heart will be also." (Matthew 6:20-21)*
66. *"Not that I seek the gift, but I seek the fruit that abounds to your account." (Philippians 4:17)*

There are also two women, describing two kingdoms in the Bible. There is the Bride of Christ, and there is Mystery Babylon the great, the Mother of Harlots. Both these kingdoms are adorned with precious stones, with good and evil intentions. The Bride's stones represent spiritual transformations of God's perfect Image, while the Harlot's stones are physical stones for the lust of wealth on earth.

67. *"Then I John, saw the holy city, New Jerusalem coming down out of Heaven from God, prepared as a bride adorned for her husband." (Revelation 21:2)*
68. *"The women was arrayed in purple and scarlet, and adorned with gold and precious stones and pearls, having in her hand a golden cup full of abominations and filthiness of her fornication. And on her forehead a name was written, Mystery Babylon the Great, the Mother of Harlots and of the Abominations of the earth." (Revelation 17:4-5)*

We must be clear that the Mother of Harlot's stones are earthly precious stones for wealth. We cannot judge and just say the stones, that are manifesting in churches around the world today, are from the devil. Her stones are said to be used for trading on the earth.

> 69. *"The kings of the earth who committed fornication and lived luxuriously with her will weep and lament for her, when they see the smoke of her burning." (Revelation 18:9)*
> 70. *"And the merchants of the earth will weep and mourn over her, for no one buys their merchandise anymore." (Revelation 18:11)*
> 71. *"Merchandise of gold and silver, precious stones and pearls, fine linen and purple, silk and scarlet, every kind of citron wood, every kind of object of ivory, every kind of object of most precious wood, iron, and marble..." (Revelation 18:12)*

The precious stones of the Bride of Christ will always carry a pure, beautiful 'mystery' for they have, throughout time on earth and in Heaven. The precious stones are the mystery of the Church, being in Christ from the foundation of the world. They speak and reveal to those who have eyes to see and blind those who are not His. For the mystery of ages is that God's grace would perfect, and polish stones that carry and shine the fullness of Him, His people, His Bride.

> 72. *"However, we speak wisdom among those who are mature, yet not the wisdom of this age, nor of the rulers of this age, who are coming to nothing. But we speak the wisdom of God in a mystery, the hidden wisdom which God ordained before the ages for our glory, which none of the rulers of this age knew, for had they known, they would not have crucified the Lord of glory." (1 Corinthians 2:6-7)*
> 73. *"This is the great mystery, but I speak concerning Christ and the Church." (Ephesians 5:32)*

The Bride of Christ is spoken of as a city, and Believers are individual living stones in the spiritual city. And all our precious stones and memorial stones will shine in the walls of salvation around us in the spiritual Temple, reflecting the full spectrum of God's fullness in glorious colours.

74. *"We have a strong city; God will appoint salvation for walls and bulwarks. Open the gates that the righteous nation, which keeps the truth, may enter in."* (Isaiah 26:1-2)

75. *"But you shall call your walls Salvation and your gates Praise."* (Isaiah 60:18)

76. *"Behold I will lay your stones with colourful gems. And lay your foundations with sapphires. I will make your pinnacles of rubies, your gates of crystal. And all your walls of precious stones."* (Isaiah 54:11-12)

77. *"The construction of its wall was jasper, and the city was pure gold, like clear glass. The foundations of the wall of the city were adorned with all kinds of precious stones, the first foundation was jasper, the second sapphire, the third chalcedony, the fourth emerald, the fifth sardonyx, the sixth sardius, the seventh chrysolite, the eighth beryl, the ninth topaz, the tenth chrysoprase, the eleventh jacinth, and the twelfth amethyst. The twelve gates were twelve pearls each individual gate was one pearl. And the street of the city was pure gold, like transparent glass."* (Revelation 21: 18-21)

The day will come when Jesus will return and bring Heaven to earth. The Temple of God will come down and manifest on earth and expel all wickedness.

78. *"Now I saw a new Heaven and a new earth, for the first Heaven and the first earth had passed away (restored). Also, there was no more sea. Then I, John saw the holy city, New Jerusalem coming down out of Heaven from God, prepared as a bride adorned for her husband. And I heard a loud voice from Heaven saying, behold, the tabernacle of God is with men, and he will dwell with them, and they shall be His people. God himself will be with them and be their God"* (Revelation 21:1-3)

79. *"And he carried me away in the Spirit to a great mountain, and showed me the great city, the holy Jerusalem, descending out of Heaven from God, having the glory of God. Her light was like a most precious stone, like a jasper stone, clear as crystal." (Revelation 21:10-11)*
80. *"But the cowardly, unbelieving, abominable, murderers, sexually immoral, sorcerers, idolaters, and all liars shall have their part in the lake which burns with fire and brimstone, which is the second death." (Revelation 21:8)*

CHAPTER TWENTY

Concluding Appeal & Whereto from Here?

Throughout this book, I have presented a case, a Biblical argument for why gemstones are manifesting around Believers today. It may seem strange to many, but the evidence is clear that the Bible is full of gemstone revelation and that they came down from Heaven.

In this book, I have

1. Explained what the gemstones phenomenon is, and how it manifests,
2. Shown Biblical Scholarship that mentions gemstones coming down from Heaven: in Jewish tradition and history.
3. Documented from Jewish Rabbi's writings & Jewish early first-century texts that they believed gemstones came down from Heaven.
4. Dealt with controversies in our age on manifesting gemstones.
5. Looked at Biblical examples of stones coming down from Heaven, Moses' stones, the Priest's Urim & Thummim stones, the stones that fell down with the manna in the wilderness,
6. Made the case, that if all other evidence was non-existent, the "Creation Covenant" argument as a Bride would establish manifesting gemstones from Heaven throughout all creation anywhere and anytime.
7. Made the appeal that priests, brides, lords, and kings were and are to be adorned with precious stones. And have given a chapter for each.
8. Explained that stones have a function of what we carry and what we have established in the Kingdom, etc. – seasons of maturing, gifting's, future rewards.
9. Shown that memorial stones in Scripture speak of "representation stones" of function, victories, rewards, and giftings.
10. Shown that the treasure of our hearts will be accounted to our Heavenly accounts, for where your heart is your treasure is also.

11. Explained that manifesting stones today are multi-dimensional revelations stones.
12. Revealed that everything that was adorned with precious stones, like Gardens, Temples, Tents, Tabernacles, and the Church (Temple) are a typology of Believers. And all Gardens, Temples, Tents, and Tabernacles were seen as brides needing to be adorned.
13. Shown the relationship of our works and our rewards being studded in the walls of salvation in the eternal city in Heaven.
14. Revealed what I believe the "Stones of Fire" were which Lucifer covered in God's heart.
15. Reflected on "teardrop" gemstones and their relationship to Scripture, as our tears are bottled up in skin-bottles in Heaven.
16. Reflected on the ecosystem that grows around our garden (souls) in the 'spirit of the kingdom', and on how Eden expands like a canopy around us and its connection to precious stones and guardian creatures.
17. Have documented the "Full Council" of Scripture on gemstones in the Bible.
18. And more…

The phenomenon of manifesting gemstones is fully Biblical and set in Jewish context!

So where do we go from here; what is the future? In one sense, the Kingdom of Heaven will just keep manifesting more and more, as it unites with its bride – creation. We will see more and more of that Heavenly Kingdom physically manifesting on earth. Those who do not like the supernatural or the reality of that Kingdom will not like Heaven, for it is coming to earth.

What is the future? I always say, if you want to know the future with God, then look at the past. Eternity is unfolding, so look back to where you are heading. As Moses walked up the mountain into the midst of the cloud, to receive his two sapphire stones (Exodus 24:10-18), this is where we are heading.

I have seen children fall into visions on the floor, and report that in Heaven, Jesus gave them a gemstone, and then, as they come back out of their visions, their empty hand closes, and they sit up and open their hand, and there is the gemstone from Heaven manifested. If that was supernatural, then what is next, is truly Biblical and supernatural.

Moses went physically into the cloud; this was not a vision. What is to happen next, is what has happened in the past: Believers will be translated fully into Heaven and back, to receive from Heaven. This might sound like too much, but this was happening in 1948, in the ministry of the Ladies of Gold, the Ministry of the Golden Candlestick.

James Maloney in his book, *Ladies of Gold: The Remarkable Ministry of the Golden Candlestick,* records what he saw at many meetings he went to:

> "All of the earthly translations and raptures were separate from the translations to Heaven, where many would return with sandals entwined with strange jewels, vest-like garments inset with twelve stones representing the tribes of Israel, headdresses arrayed in almost living colours, articles of clothing that would be stitched with gold thread – I mean the metal, not the colour…these encounters were constant for over fifty years, straight from day one when they gathered together…I recall seeing a door in that sanctuary, beautifully moulded, emanating a golden hue. I assumed when people walked through it, it led to another part of the house. Many years later, when walking through the house…I was stunned to realise the door was not there. It was explained to me that the door was a special door to Heaven. I didn't bother

asking for further details – they wouldn't have been provided anyway."¹

Jesus said if you can believe "*All things are Possible*". (Mark 9:23)

"The stones cry out, long silent through the ages,
unfolding now, a written scroll, God's truth in dusty pages.
The stones cry out, their story tells with power,
long hidden from the eyes of man, God's truth for this hour."

(Anne Moore)²

---

[1] James Maloney, Ladies Of Gold: The Remarkable Ministry Of The Golden Candlestick, WestBow Press, 2011, p.9
[2] Randall Price, The Stones cry Out, World of Bible Ministries, Inc 1997, p.1

BIBLIOGRAPHY

Abbot, S. (Jul 2018), *Reasons for Hope: A Stone of Deliverance and memorial in Joshua* – Retrieved July 2019 from https://reasonsforhopejesus.com/7-stone-deliverance-memorial-joshua/

Abrahams, Justin Paul (2016) *Beyond Human*, Seraph Creative

Alec, W. (2005) *The Fall of Lucifer*. Warboys Publishing Ltd

Alec, W. (2013) *Visions of Heaven*. Warboys Publishing Ltd

Alport, O. (February 2019). *Was There Enough – or too much?* Retrieved June 2019, from https://hamodia.com/columns/was-there-enough-or-too-much/

Arns, M. David (2014) *Gold Dust, Jewels, & More: Manifestations of God*.

Beale, G.K (2004) *The Temple and the Church's Mission*. InterVarsity Press.

Beale, S. Stephen Beale, (Nov 2017) *Why do Christians Get White Stones in Heaven?* Retrieved June 2019 from https://catholicexchange.com/christians-get-white-stones-heaven

Clayton, I. (2016), *Realms of the Kingdom, Volume Two*. Sons of Thunder Publications.

Crowder, J. (2009) *The Ecstasy of Loving God*. Destiny Image Publishers.

Cruz, L (2007) *All His Jewels: From Glory to Glory*. Xulon Press.

Curtis, A. (2019) *Talk With Me in Paradise*. Kin & Kingdom Books.

Dye, D. (2016) *The Temple in Creation: A Portrait of the Family*. Foundations in Torah Publishing.

Dye, D. (2015) *The Temple in The Garden: Priests and Kings*. Foundations in Torah Publishing.

Edwards, J. (2005) *Charity and Its Fruit*. The Banner of Truth Trust.

Enklin, A. (2015 January), *Living Torah: Leaving Egypt and Looking to the Future*. Retrieved June 25, 2019 from http://Unitedwithisrael.org/living-torah-leaving-egypt-and-looking-to-the-future/

Gallups, C. (2018) *Gods of Ground Zero, The Truth of Eden's Iniquity*. Defender Publishing

Hardinge, L. (2011) *Stones OF Fire*. American Christian Ministries.

Healy, B. K. (2018) *The Veil: An Invitation to the Unseen Realm*, Charisma House.

Heiser, S. M. (2015) *The Unseen Realm: Recovering the supernatural worldview of the Bible*, Lexham Press.

Ilani, Z. *Diamonds and Gemstones in Judaica*. Published by Harry Oppenheimer Diamond Museum.

Lisorkin Eyzenberg, E., Retrieved June 2019, from https://israelbiblicalstudies.com/bible-jewish-studies/#bible-studies

King, C. M. (2016) *Gemstones from Heaven*, Self-Published.

Maloney, J. (2011) *Ladies of Gold: The Remarkable Ministry Of The Golden Candlestick*. WestBow Press.

Missler, Chuck (2000) Chuck Missler, *Hidden Treasures in the Biblical Text*. Koinonia House

Mouliert, G. (2011) *The Breastplate of the High Priest: Unlocking the Mystery of the Living Stones*. Keeper Publishing.

Neusner, J. (2001) *A Theological Commentary to the Midrash: Song of Song Rabbat*

Pease, G. (2014) *The Jewels of Heaven*. Retrieved June 2019 from https://sermons.faithlife.com/sermons/124750-the-jewels-of-heaven

Pitre, B. (2014) *Jesus the Bridegroom: The Greatest Love Story Ever Told.* Crown Publishing.

Prempeh-Dapaah, A. (2018) *Laying Up Treasures in Heaven*, Stonewall Press

Price, Paula A., PhD. (2014) *Before the Garden: God's Eternal Continuum.* Flaming Vision Publications

Price, R. (1997) *The Stones cry Out.* World of Bible Ministries Inc

Rosenfeld, D. (n.d.) *Urim and Thummim*. Retrieved June 2019 from https://www.aish.com/atr/Urim-and-Thummim.html.

Smith, G. & T. (2014) *Gemstones from Heaven.* Netturtle Studios Publishing.

Stone, P. (2015) *Chronicles Of The Sacred Mountain*. Voice of Evangelism Outreach Ministries.

Storms, S. (n.d.) *The Letter To The Church At Pergamum (2:12-17)*. Retrieved June 2019 from https://www.samstorms.com/all-articles/post/the-letter-to-the-church-at-pergamum--2:12-17-

Trask, M. (2009) *The 12 Gemstones of Revelation: Unlocking the Significance of the Gemstones Phenomenon*. Destiny Image Publishers.

Wilkinson, B. (2002), *A Life God Rewards: Why Everything You Do Today Matters Forever*, Multnomah Publishers, Inc.

www.ingramcontent.com/pod-product-compliance
Lightning Source LLC
Chambersburg PA
CBHW031418290426
44110CB00011B/434